D0966470

A Man
Named Tony

The True Story of the
Yablonski Murders

———

A Man
Named Tony

By Stuart Brown

W·W·NORTON & COMPANY·INC·

NEW YORK

First Edition

THIS BOOK *was typeset in RCA VideoComp Times Roman, a computer-assisted photocomposition process. Composition, printing, and binding were done by the Kingsport Press.*

Library of Congress Cataloging in Publication Data
Brown, Stuart.
    A man named Tony.
    Includes index.
    1. Boyle, William A. 2. Yablonski, Joseph. I. Title.
KF224.B68B76   364.1'523'0924 [B]   75–20280

ISBN 0 393 08707 7

1 2 3 4 5 6 7 8 9

For my wife,
ELLEN FAWCETT BROWN

Contents

Photographs appear following page 103

A Man
Named Tony

1

The Odor of Death

THE HOUSE REEKED. When the police arrived, they were hit with the smell, malodorous, pervasive, of rotting human flesh. It almost floored Elmer Schifko, a big, beefy Pennsylvania state policeman, a veteran of such discoveries. He had to fight off the urge to vomit. If ever there was a time for a cigarette, he thought, this was it. Elmer Schifko fought that off, too. One of his companions considered sending for gas masks, but there was no time for that, either. From the second floor of the graystone farmhouse to the kitchen, whose temperature was still set at eighty degrees this cool January afternoon, there was police work to do.

In the two bedrooms, Glen Werking and Robert Dugan, two other Pennsylvania state policemen, combed through the blood-soaked mattresses, searching for bullets. Dr. Ernest Abernathy, a pathologist, used his penlight to examine the bullet holes in the three bodies. The coroner, Farrell Jackson, inspected the bedrooms and the bodies with less than his usual aplomb: Jackson had been a coal miner and he had known two of the deceased for thirty-five years. Jackson looked at the daughter, the curlers still in her hair, and sobbed. "The work of a maniac," he said.

Everybody noticed how the house reeked. "The odor of death," Kenneth Yablonski, a lawyer usually given to precise terminology, called it. But that was a phrase Ken Yablonski used much later, in relative tranquility. Now, he put his hands over his face and wept harder than anyone else. Ken Yablonski's father and stepmother and stepsister were dead—their bodies riddled with a total of nine bullets—and he was the first to find them in the graystone farmhouse that stank of their decomposed flesh.

It was the morning of January 5, 1970. Ken Yablonski was growing concerned. Some friends of his father's were attending a swearing-in ceremony for a local judge. All over Pennsylvania, this Monday, January 5, was Inauguration Day for mayors, judges, and other officials who had been elected the previous November. But Ken Yablonski's father, long active in Washington County and Pennsylvania politics, did not show up at the county courthouse for the ceremonies. His father had lost a different kind of election himself several weeks before, but his failure to show up even for the reception was strange.

Ken hadn't seen his family since Christmas. It occurred to him that they might have gone to Bethesda, Maryland, where his stepbrother, Joseph, Jr., lived. Ken's calls to his father's house in Clarksville went unanswered, but he figured that they were indeed away and would be back after the first of the year.

When his father didn't appear at the ceremonies, Ken decided to drive to the farmhouse in Clarksville. He took a friend with him. They drove over the back roads of Washington County that Ken knew so well from having grown up, lived, and practiced law there—over southwestern Pennsylvania's hills and valleys dotted with coal fields and clear springs and even a few unspoiled forests. At the southern edge of the county, they reached the borough of Clarksville and his father's house, just a few hundred feet from the county line. It was a quiet January day, but the closer they got to the house, the more Ken Yablonski became concerned. He hadn't seen his family for a week, and he had learned only this Inauguration Day that they were not in Bethesda.

Ken had a key to the door the family always used. He went into the house the customary way and therefore didn't notice the jammed-open door at the side of the house—the calling card of strangers who had been inside. In a courtroom nearly two years later, Kenneth Yablonski spewed out the details of what he found that eleventh day of Christmas:

"When I got to the top of the steps and looked toward the bedrooms on the right, I saw what appeared to be a very large body laying on the bed completely covered by, like, a quilt, a bedspread or something like that. I ran into the room. It looked too large to be my mother. I thought it was my father, or I didn't know really, and the face was covered as though they pulled the cover over their face.

"I took the cover and I pulled it back. I couldn't see the face because it was all black or dark. But I could see the long hair and that's when I realized it was my mother. I looked for my father. I didn't see him on the bed. There were some times he snored or that sort of thing; they would sleep in separate bedrooms, so I thought maybe he was in another bedroom.

"I ran out of that bedroom and ran into what used to be my brother's and my bedroom. I ran into there looking for my father and I saw my sister.

"She was laying face down on the bed right next to the door and there was just blood all over the bed. It was just all around and her body was sort of dark in color, and as I could see her legs, I remember the blood all over the bed.

"As I was looking—I was still looking for my father—I remember saying, 'Where's my dad? Where is he? What did they do to him?' I don't know whether I went into the other bedroom or not.

"Then I ran back, this time all the way in my parents' bedroom and down around the bed. At this time I saw my father. He was off on the other side of the bed. My mother was on the near side closest to the door.

"He was off the bed in almost like a kneeling, collapsed sort of position . . . propped up against, I think, the end table. I'm not sure. I remember seeing a lot of blood, looked like blood. I remember seeing a spot. . . . He had an undershirt on, and

I just looked. I don't know that I did anything else, and then I ran out of the room and I ran downstairs."

Within an hour, word came over wire-service teletype machines across the nation:

THE UNSUCCESSFUL CANDIDATE FOR PRESIDENT OF THE UNITED MINE WORKERS OF AMERICA, JOSEPH YABLONSKI, HAS BEEN FOUND DEAD, ALONG WITH HIS WIFE AND DAUGHTER, AT HIS HOME IN CLARKSVILLE, PENNSYLVANIA. STATE POLICE SAY YABLONSKI WAS MURDERED.

And at the courthouse in Washington County, the reception for the judge broke up when Farrell Jackson came running into the hotel with the words: "Jock's dead! Jock Yablonski's dead!"

The three Yablonskis had been dead for several days, giving the killers plenty of time to flee. The house was in a remote corner of southwestern Pennsylvania, not far from both the Ohio and West Virginia borders, so the assassins must have known how to find the house. They had cut the telephone wires, all but the one phone Ken Yablonski had been ringing without getting either an answer or a disconnect signal. And in the driveway, they had disabled two cars, belonging to Yablonski and his daughter. The break-in at the house was simple. The killers had removed a storm door from the side of the house that the family seldom used, and then merely opened the unlocked inside door. All they had to do then was to make their way up to the second-floor bedrooms by the reflected glare of an outside floodlight. But the clues were scarce—at first.

And the killings were brutal. Joseph Yablonski had five shells pumped into him; his wife Margaret, two; their daughter Charlotte, still wearing her hair curlers, also two. The husband and wife were in one bedroom and the daughter in another, indicating that all three had been asleep when the killers broke in and surprised them.

In the house, they left behind one living thing—a dog named Rascal, who yelped, scrambled and tore up newspapers, and foraged among the Christmas decorations for days on end, until Ken Yablonski came to the house and found the animal still alive.

By three o'clock in the afternoon, a small army of reporters, photographers, television crews, coal miners, and police had descended on the farmhouse in Clarksville. Many of the twelve hundred citizens of the borough were there too, gawking at the comings and goings of gray-uniformed state policemen in green cars. Heads turned skyward to watch a helicopter circling, its passenger filming aerial views of the hilly terrain and the drive-way and the disabled cars and the house where the odor of death, despite a few opened windows now, was still overwhelming.

On the patio in the knot of people who were permitted near the doorway, a miner from West Virginia whispered to a news-man what he had just told a state policeman—that a suspicious car from Ohio had been at the house a few weeks before.

At seven o'clock that night, thousands of television sets in southwestern Pennsylvania, northern West Virginia, and east-ern Ohio were tuned to Channel 2 out of Pittsburgh, for the latest word on the Yablonski murders. A solemn, dark-haired anchorman, eyes glistening, intoned the words of the top story of the evening:

"Joseph 'Jock' Yablonski, whose controversial career in the coal fields around the country had spanned some forty years, was found shot to death today, along with his wife and daughter. . . . Autopsies on all three bodies are now being performed in Washington, Pennsylvania. . . .

"A United Mine Workers Union spokesman in Washington said late today that the incumbent president of the United Mine Workers Union, W. A. 'Tony' Boyle, was—quote—'shocked and flabbergasted' when he learned of the shootings late today.

Edward Carey, legal counsel for the UMW, said that he was sure the shootings had nothing to do with the election or the United Mine Workers Union.

"Carey said that Boyle, who was unavailable for comment himself, was so upset when he heard the news that he immediately went home."

And then, on videotape, but with an eerie quality so real that it appeared the man on the tube was alive there in the studio— came the craggy face, the soft blue eyes, the pugnacious nose, and the low voice made hoarse from six months of campaigning against Tony Boyle for the presidency of the United Mine Workers of America. Jock Yablonski was on the tube again, speaking as he had ten days before in an interview with four high-school kids, speaking about how he had been beaten by Tony Boyle on December 8, but not speaking like a loser. Jock Yablonski was speaking about the "southern district" of the United Mine Workers, districts that embraced parts of Tennessee, Kentucky, and Alabama, places where he had feared to wage his campaign. Yablonski was speaking about the poverty and hopelessness that were epidemic in the union's southern regions, and of union leaders' promises to the poor of the Appalachian coal fields. Over the television set, the hoarse voice and blue eyes seemed to be alive again as the man groped for words.

"In some of the areas of the southern jurisdictions," Yablonski was telling the high-school kids, "these people are really in despair. And if it's not coal mining down there, it's public assistance. There's never been any action with reference to getting any diversification in the area. . . . They've heard politicians promise them before. And I think that they spell this thing out the same way—that these are just election promises, and mean nothing."

The videotape of Jock Yablonski's last public words faded to a moment of discrete, soundless black on the television screen, and Yablonski's fighting was over for good.

At the house in Clarksville, the sun had gone down but the Pennsylvania state police were still working. Officers Dugan and Werking had recovered seven spent bullets from the bedrooms—three of them in the blood-soaked mattresses—and other men had found two cartons of milk at the kitchen door, six newspapers, and an aluminum molding that had been removed from the side of the storm door. The milk was sour, the newspapers had piled up since December 31, and the door and the molding had yielded no fingerprints.

After eight o'clock, a reporter and photographer went to the Washington Hospital at the county seat, to try to find out what the autopsy showed about the time of death and the number of shots and the nature of the wounds. As they turned a corner of the third floor of the hospital, they were hit by the same smell that had nearly overwhelmed the police at the farmhouse earlier in the day. The odor of death. The two men glimpsed three stretchers, a body on each. Only policemen or doctors look at such sights carefully. The pair took one glance at the terrible purple and black blobs before them and turned on their heels. The photographer uttered one word: "Why?"

Dr. Abernathy's autopsies at the hospital morgue lasted until well after midnight. After removing the curlers from Charlotte Yablonski's hair, he found two gunshot wounds of the top of the head. In the body of her mother, he found a wound of the right shoulder that pierced the pulmonary artery, and another of the left collarbone. Jock Yablonski, he noted, had very little hardening of the arteries for a man of fifty-nine who was obese, but there were five bullet wounds in the body, including the one that Dr. Abernathy called the *coup de grâce*. That was the one that entered the back of Yablonski's skull.

Dr. Abernathy estimated that the three Yablonskis had been dead between four and seven days. He also recovered five more bullets.

The funeral was held on Friday, four days after the discov-

ery of the bodies, at the Immaculate Conception Church, a
graystone building on a commanding hill a couple of blocks
from the Washington County Courthouse. All week long, state
police and county officers had fanned out over southwestern
Pennsylvania, seeking clues, interviewing every resident of the
borough of Clarksville (population twelve hundred), going as
far north as Pittsburgh, down into West Virginia and west into
Ohio. They contacted coal miners, and checked telephone company records and searched the house of death. They interviewed
and reinterviewed Kenneth Yablonski, who was joined now by
his brother Joseph, Jr., from Bethesda, the younger son of Jock,
not yet thirty, whom everybody called Chip. The police noted
the comings and goings of thousands of persons at the small
funeral home in Millsboro, near Clarksville, where the caskets
stood before the ceremony at the church.

Nearly a thousand persons were drawn to the church for
what was no ordinary rite. In some respects, it was a subdued
political rally, for hundreds of supporters of Jock Yablonski
appeared, and leaders of the United Mine Workers, whom Yablonski had fought for most of the previous year, were told by
his family not to come—nor to send flowers.

That Friday of the funeral was one of the bitterest winter
days that anyone could remember in southwestern Pennsylvania. Snow covered the ground, and an incessant gusty wind
whipped the air to what seemed like thirty degrees below zero,
though the actual temperature hovered at one below. It was so
cold that movie cameras froze and new cars broke down, and
the earth in the Washington cemetery was so hard it would have
required a bulldozer to turn the ground. Frozen mourners coming into the church huddled gratefully together while their bodies warmed each other.

The political note at the Mass of the Resurrection was
sounded by a politically active priest of the Roman Catholic
Church, Monsignor Charles Owen Rice of Pittsburgh. Once,
this had been his church, and he had known Jock Yablonski
for many years, had married him and Margaret, and had fellow-

traveled with him in union circles, for Rice was known as an outspoken labor priest.

Wearing white vestments, the symbol of hope in death, Rice stood at the transept as concelebrant of the Mass and looked out over an audience that was still stunned by the enormity of the tragedy represented in the three caskets before them. The caskets were awash in the light of television cameras, whose positions Rice had arranged at a somber briefing the night before.

The priest paid particular attention to Kenneth and Chip Yablonski, sitting on the front row. He saw in their faces both fear and determination. Fear was on everyone's face. Joseph L. Rauh, Jr., the Washington, D.C., lawyer who had represented Yablonski in the union election campaign, bore the countenance of fear, and so did white-haired Elmer Brown, from West Virginia, who had been Yablonski's running mate for vice president. Three West Virginia doctors who had fought both the union and the coal operators were afraid, despite the solidarity of the multitude in the church, and so was Congressman Ken Hechler, a scholarly West Virginia Democrat who had been the only congressman openly to help Yablonski's cause while he was alive. Scores of anonymous miners were in the church, too, and though fear nagged at them, they drew a measure of courage —as did everyone—when Father Rice began to speak.

The white-clad priest, a balding man with a lilting brogue and an optimistic twinkle, articulated the full meaning of Jock Yablonski's death—and spoke the word that was on everyone's fearful mind.

"Assassination," Rice said. He noted that the 1960s, newly ended, had produced the killings of John Kennedy, Robert Kennedy, and Martin Luther King. "But this was worse," he told the mourners, gazing down on the three caskets. "In this, there was the element of cold-blooded preparation. And how chilling and efficient it must have been—the premeditated murder of two women. We are hardened in this country, but this is something new to us. This action, no matter what the motive, is disturbing and evil, beyond words to describe. Why, we ask—why, and who?"

The funeral procession moved over the snow-covered hills outside the town to the Washington cemetery. Going up the packed snow on the hills, some of the cars got stuck, their tires squealing madly as they failed to make the road up to the entrance to the graveyard. Other cars detoured around the stalled ones, and the procession halted at one of the highest peaks in the county. The elderly among the mourners huddled under a makeshift tent, seeking shelter from the icy gusts and stamping their feet in the granitelike snow. The burial ceremony was performed unhurriedly, while police in civilian clothes unobtrusively scrutinized the crowd for possible suspects.

Afterward a hundred men, led by attorney Rauh and Yablonski's neighbor Mike Trbovich, met in the cafeteria of the Immaculate Conception School and decided to do what they had to do—continue Jock Yablonski's fight against the union. They were still fearful, but they were going on, as coal miners do. Their memorial to Jock Yablonski would be to continue his fight against Tony Boyle.

The Pennsylvania state police held daily briefings with the press but reported little of note. The investigation, however, was going on, with a number of leads on a number of fronts. The police now pinpointed the time of the shootings—the Yablonskis had been dead for more than five days at the time of Ken Yablonski's discovery. The winds whipped the graystone farmhouse in Clarksville, and as the days passed, few tourists came by. Newsmen began to leave the area, too, as it became obvious that there would be no immediate arrests.

Soon, the farmhouse was boarded up and locked, and the Yablonski case began to leave the front pages and the nightly newscasts. The severed telephone wires and the disabled two cars in the driveway at the farmhouse yielded no clues; and the seven spent shells recovered inside showed no fingerprints, but the police weren't telling all they knew.

For, on the day after Ken Yablonski met the odor of death, Pennsylvania Trooper Glen Werking found the first clue, in the den on the first floor. In Jock Yablonski's desk was a yellow legal-sized notepad, and Werking, leafing through its pages, came upon some scrawlings in the hand of the dead man. There was an Ohio auto license number and a telephone number and some other writings, including two names; all adding up to the fact that the man now in the frozen ground of the Washington cemetery had pointed the way to his assassins.

"I Shall Die an Honest Man"

RALPH NADER stood at the rear of the hotel room. There was a crowd of reporters, photographers, and television crews on hand for a media event at the Mayflower Hotel in Washington, D.C. It was the morning of May 29, 1969, and though Nader had helped attract the news media representatives to the hotel, he stayed out of the limelight. He was there to lend his imprimatur to another man's cause.

It was Jock Yablonski's morning, and he brought along his son Chip, a nephew, and his lawyer. He was going to announce his break with the United Mine Workers of America, an organization he had served loyally for more than forty years. It seemed a foolhardy, even dangerous thing to do, and Jock's son and nephew, both over six feet tall, stood at the door in case there was any trouble. The year 1969 was a presidential election year in the union, and Jock was going to tell the world that he would oppose Tony Boyle for the top position in the nearly two-hundred-thousand-member union.

Only a few newsmen realized the importance of the story, and those who did had difficulty selling it to their editors—except in the coal fields, where taking on the union establishment was like coming out against God. Tony Boyle had become president of the United Mine Workers in 1963, claiming inheritance from the mighty John L. Lewis, had been elected to a five-year term in 1964, and had made it clear that spring of 1969 that he would brook no serious opposition in his bid for another full term. Yablonski had unsuccessfully sought the union vice presidency in 1964, claiming a solid power base in Pennsylvania, and had been punished by Boyle in 1966 by being removed as president of the Pittsburgh-based District 5 of the union. If Yablonski had any reservations about Boyle's leadership after that, he kept his mouth shut—until May 29, 1969.

Now he read a lengthy statement, which Nader had helped him write, and it was a ringing declaration of defiance against an organization Yablonski regarded as a dictatorship ruled by corrupt men.

"In an otherwise harsh and hostile environment," declared Yablonski, "the miners relied on their union, trusted their union, and gave the union their undivided loyalty. But in recent years, the present leadership has not responded to its men, has not fought for their health and safety, has not improved grievance procedures, has not rooted itself in the felt needs of its membership, and the right of rank-and-file participation in the small and large issues that affect the union.

"I have been part of this leadership. I participated in and tolerated the deteriorating performance of this leadership—but with increasingly troubled conscience. I will no longer be beholden to the past. I can no longer tolerate the low state to which our union has fallen."

Yablonski went on to offer an eleven-point platform. It ranged from expanding the union's mine-safety activities (which were almost nil in the most dangerous occupation in America) to ending the practice of having international headquarters appoint district officers. The rank and file, he said, would elect its own officers under his presidency. Yablonski promised an "open administration," participatory democracy, no relatives on the payroll, and said he would keep the coal companies at arm's length.

He was looking ahead to a vigorous campaign, and he was not unmindful of the risks. He remembered how dissidents had been beaten bloody on the floor of the union's convention in

Miami in 1964. Their crime: they had dared to speak out for election of district officers. And Yablonski knew it would be a long campaign—longer than the previous year's campaign for the presidency of the United States. He was fifty-nine years old and in good health, but he would need all his strength and all the help he could get to overturn the union establishment. The union sprawled over twenty-four districts in more than half the United States and Canada, and there were places he couldn't campaign personally—Kentucky and Tennessee, for example, where they lavished praise on Tony Boyle and were likely to greet anti-Boyle strangers with shotguns.

Jock Yablonski wouldn't campaign in the southern union districts of Appalachia, but he was still confident he could whip Tony Boyle in an honest election.

The stakes in the election were high, not only for the candidates, but for the working coal miners, the newly rejuvenated coal industry, and the public. If a rebel movement could overturn an established union leadership, that would produce shock waves throughout organized labor, which had become fat and complacent since the merger of the AFL and the CIO in 1955. That was one reason Ralph Nader helped Jock Yablonski make his break with the Boyle administration.

Only a week before the Mayflower Hotel press conference, Nader sent a letter to John L. Lewis at the retired union president's home in Alexandria, Virginia. It was strong medicine for the ailing eighty-nine-year-old Lewis. It charged that the union he had guided with an iron hand into the forefront of the American labor movement was now in the hands of a bunch of egotistical dictators. Forgotten, said Nader, were the health and safety needs of one hundred twenty thousand miners.

"Incompetence, sinecurism, waste, remoteness from the rank and file, misuse of union funds and violations of democratic electoral procedures in an epidemic manner have become a way of life for W. A. Boyle's administration," said Nader. "Mr. Boyle has encouraged and demanded a saturation campaign of hero-worship and adulation that is characterized by an intensity comparable only to authoritarian or totalitarian rulers of various foreign nations."

Nader warned Lewis that Boyle was trying to displace Lewis as chairman of the union's Welfare and Retirement Fund, in order to manipulate the fund to insure Boyle's reelection. Nader told Lewis that he should "resist any attempts to displace you and that, more, you should reject any effort to obtain your approval or acquiescence regarding the deplorable and self-serving leadership of the UMW and their disgraceful policies or non-policies."

Nader never got a reply from John L. Lewis, because within two weeks of Yablonski's announcement of candidacy, John L. Lewis was dead.

He left behind a union that was being torn apart at a time when its members needed leadership most—a time of a healthy resurgence in coal as a force in the American economy. The coal bin in the home and the smoke-belching train were long gone in America, but coal was once again becoming "black gold," and the men who risked life and limb every day to mine it were overdue for a share of the nuggets. In the late 1960s, the coal industry actually entered a boom time, and there were fat profits to be wrung out of mine fields of Appalachia, the Midwest, and the far West. The prize was low-sulfur bituminous (so-called "soft" coal, which is the least polluting). Its richest veins cut a wide, peninsulalike swath from northwestern Pennsylvania, through West Virginia and Ohio, southwestward through eastern Kentucky, Tennessee, and northern Alabama. There, the bulk of the working and retired members of the UMW lived, the working men going to their dark, dangerous tasks underground each day, the pensioners eking out a meager existence with a monthly stipend of $115 and a hospital card that, like the pension, could be rendered nonexistent by a stroke of the pen at international headquarters of the union in Washington. Working or retired, they were peons.

But the stake in coal—for the operators and owners—

became enormous in the late 1960s. Although there were some seven thousand private operators in the business, much of the industry, by the late 1960s, was effectively controlled by a few noncoal giant corporations. The second-largest coal company, Consolidation Coal, was acquired in 1966 by Continental Oil (itself the ninth biggest oil company). Consol, as it is known in the industry, showed 1972 profits of more than $170 million, in the same year that its parent-company officers were able to raise five million dollars for Richard Nixon's reelection, during a single dinner in Houston. Consol produces more than sixty million tons of coal a year and owns more than seven billion tons in reserves. In 1968, the largest coal company, Peabody, was acquired by Kennecott Copper, despite a government challenge in the courts. That action placed a vast hoard of western U.S. coal at the disposal of a huge multinational corporation. And the third-largest coal producer, Island Creek, was purchased by Occidental Petroleum in 1968 with accumulated capital from oil operations in Libya. A so-called "favorable tax ruling" enabled Occidental to avoid paying taxes on the purchase. Aside from these giants, other corporations such as United States Steel, as well as electric utilities and chemical firms, own what are known as "captive" mines—coal produced for their own use.

Before the dawning of what came to be known as the energy crisis, U.S. coal exports had nearly doubled in a decade, one reason being the emergence of Japan as a coal-hungry producer of steel. In the United States, the power blackouts of the late 1960s dramatized the need for more electrical power, and low-sulfur coal, when it could be found, helped meet the demands of the energy situation and the environmentalists. It was no wonder, then, that West Virginia, the largest coal-producing state (as well as one of the poorest) was called one vast billion-dollar coal field. The state was said to have enough coal to continue mining for the next four hundred years.

For a steady flow of profits, the coal industry, mechanized

since after the Second World War, required what was euphemistically called "labor peace." The coal companies were always blaming wildcat strikes and low productivity for their economic ills. What was needed was no prolonged strikes and a complaisant union leadership. Some working miners had a blunter phrase for it: They said their leaders were in bed with the coal operators. By 1950, when it appeared that the coal industry was dying an irreversible death—hundreds of thousands of jobs had disappeared as the nation turned toward oil and gas—John L. Lewis was willing and able to guarantee labor peace. Operators of bituminous coal fields agreed to pay a forty-cent-a-ton royalty into the union's welfare fund, and that gave Lewis a sweetener for the constricting job market. Never again while he was president of the UMW did the union make serious waves in the industry. In fact, it sometimes used its swollen treasury to help bail out financially pressed managements.

Lewis became a white-maned patriarch, a shadow of the shaggy-browed martinet who had defied presidents of the United States, the Supreme Court, and the rest of the labor movement. In 1935, Lewis, angry over the supineness of the craft unions, had helped found the Congress of Industrial Organizations. His union helped bring into being such giants as the United Steelworkers and the United Auto Workers. Then, in 1942, after working unsuccessfully against President Roosevelt's third term, Lewis led the United Mine Workers out of the CIO. In 1946, his union rejoined the American Federation of Labor, but the rapprochement lasted only two years. When most labor leaders agreed to a non-Communist oath in the Taft-Hartley Act, Lewis balked, and the mine workers left the organized labor movement for good.

By 1960, Lewis, eighty years old and ready for president-emeritus status, yielded his forty-year grip as undisputed ruler of the UMW. His immediate successor was Thomas Kennedy, a former lieutenant governor of Pennsylvania, but Tony Boyle's supporters claimed that Boyle was really the one groomed for

Lewis's mantle. When Kennedy died in 1963, Boyle stepped up from vice-president to president, and he won a five-year term in the union election of 1964.

Lewis could inspire men or make them quake in their shoes; he was like some fossil fuel wrenched out of the bowels of the earth. Tony Boyle was short, balding, cautious, spoke often with averted eyes, produced affidavits to back up his statements, and was the consummate organization man. Boyle had worked his way up from the Montana coal fields to international union headquarters in Washington, and though not as flamboyant as Lewis, he shared the patriarch's dictatorial bent. Few union people ever addressed him as anything other than "President Boyle."

Under Boyle's stewardship in the 1960s, it soon became clear that the labor peace fashioned by Lewis in the 1950s was not going to be disturbed by the new administration. Indeed, the union maintained a low profile in the labor movement. The Department of the Interior, the government agency that was often regarded as a handmaiden of the mineral interests, even became more militant than the union over the issue of safety in the coal mines. The Teamsters and the Longshoremen, whose corruptions led to new labor laws, were being reformed from without, but it was business as usual inside the United Mine Workers.

On taking office, Boyle, like any politician, set about consolidating his power over the one hundred twenty thousand working miners and eighty thousand pensioners. He kept most of the union's twenty-four districts in so-called trusteeships, meaning the members wouldn't be permitted to vote for their district officers. The men he appointed to head these districts in turn became the legal authority for carrying out his policies— the union's policy-making international executive board. (In 1964, the federal government began a challenge to the trustee-ship arrangement, but the case was not actively pursued for many years.)

Another source of Boyle's hold on the union was in the

strength of its retired members. The pensioners were full voting members of the union, the only sizable block that could be manipulated by a stroke of the pen—say, through a pension increase. That's exactly what Boyle was able to do during the union campaign against Yablonski in 1969. And Boyle's administration could do more than that; international headquarters could decide whether a miner even qualified for a pension, and if he was turned down there was no appeal.

Finally, there was the union treasury, swollen to record proportions despite the declining job market in coal. The union assets alone once reached nearly $90 million. The supposedly independent Welfare and Retirement Fund, fueled by the royalty on each ton of union-mined coal, had assets of more than $150 million. Astonishingly, more than $30 million of the fund's assets were in a checking account that paid no interest—in a bank owned by the union itself. What happened to all the union's money was one of the major thrusts of Jock Yablonski's 1969 campaign to oust Tony Boyle.

A short man with a bull neck, Yablonski was as gritty as the miners he worked with. Like Boyle, Yablonski had worked in the mines as a boy. He had seen his immigrant father killed in a mine explosion, had moved up through the business side of the union, and had even been known to put a relative or two on the payroll (though by no means to the extent Boyle had, whose daughter and brother were earning more than $65,000 a year combined, on the union payroll in Montana).

Yablonski rose to become president of the UMW's District 5. Headquartered in Pittsburgh and with a membership of about fifteen thousand, the district was one of the few that was permitted to elect its own officers, instead of having them appointed from Washington. Yablonski was also elected to the UMW's international executive board, and as he approached the age of sixty, he seemed headed toward a comfortable retirement at his farmhouse in southwestern Pennsylvania.

But in the late spring of 1969, Jock Yablonski had a kind

of Saul-on-the-road-to-Damascus conversion. Perhaps it was triggered by the 1968 union convention, eight months earlier in Denver, where Boyle supporters and enforcers known as "white hats" (because they wore white hats) imposed discipline on the twenty-five hundred delegates while Boyle's minions spent $100,000 on such trinkets as inscribed cigarette lighters for the conventioneers. Perhaps it was the mining disaster two months after the convention, when seventy-eight men were trapped and given up for dead at Consol's Number 9 mine in Farmington, West Virginia, and the appearance of President Boyle at the company store, assuaging widows and mothers with the thought that, well, Consol had a pretty good safety record. (While in Washington, Interior Secretary Stewart Udall cried, "We have all been too complacent!")

Or perhaps Jock Yablonski finally became sickened by the slavish cult of personality that was built up around Tony Boyle, an outpouring that escalated as the union's 1969 election campaign approached. There was the union official who delivered encomiums to President Boyle that might have made even the great John L. blush.

"Tony Boyle has been president of this union for six years, and I want to say without fear of contradiction from anyone, anywhere in the world, he has moved the mine workers of America forward to a greater degree in a six-year period of time than any other president of any other labor organization anywhere in the world.

"There is no man anywhere in this country with greater dedication to the well-being of the United Mine Workers of America than your distinguished president, W. A. Tony Boyle.

"This dynamic union of yours has been reawakened. It's on the move and we're going forward under this great leadership of President Boyle and his distinguished officers.

"In 1963, a young man came on the scene as the president of our union—our very distinguished president, W. A. Tony Boyle. This young man [Boyle was sixty-one at the time] started to move this union forward with his dynamic manner. Pensions have been improved [in 1969, anthracite workers on pension received thirty dollars a month from the union] . . . and there are many things yet to come for the membership of our union."

Jock Yablonski may have been sickened by such words of fealty, because all of them were his own. He paid his obeisance to Tony Boyle in a series of speeches in the early spring of 1969. The speeches were recorded by the union, and gleefully handed out in phonograph-record form when Yablonski decided to run against President Boyle.

Boyle knew early in 1969 that he would face at least token opposition in the international union election, scheduled for December of that year. But he always insisted that he was surprised by Yablonski's announcement of candidacy. As Yablonski mulled things over, between weekend speeches for Boyle, he took only a few relatives and close friends into his confidence. Yablonski figured that his chances of upsetting Boyle were good, because the Yablonski power base in Pennsylvania and West Virginia embraced an area where about half the working miners live.

Yablonski was still giving speeches for Boyle early in April when the union president made Yablonski an offer he dared not refuse. Boyle wanted Yablonski to come to Washington to become acting director of the union's lobbying agency, known as Labor's Non-Partisan League. Although it required him to move to the capital, thereby putting him out of contact with his power base and supporters in District 5 in Pennsylvania, it was a well-paying job and an important one. One of the major tasks of the union that year was to press for a revision of the loopholes in the Coal Mine Health and Safety Act, and in the wake of the Farmington mine disaster, demands for new laws were incessant.

Yablonski accepted the offer on May 4, 1969. He said he'd need a couple of weeks to get his affairs in order back in Pennsylvania. Three and a half weeks later, he threw down the gauntlet to Boyle at his press conference at the Mayflower Hotel.

At UMW headquarters at 900 Fifteenth Street, a few blocks

from the White House, the reaction to the Yablonski candidacy was near-panic. No one could remember when a serious battle had been fought over the presidency of the union, and this was going to be serious, the incumbents agreed, unless some counterinsurgency was developed. Only once during John L. Lewis's reign had there been a heated battle for the leadership, and that was in the 1920s. There was no precedent for handling such a situation, and the attacks on the union by Ralph Nader and from within by a group of dissidents in membership-rich West Virginia made the task of opposing Yablonski even more difficult. Another consideration was that the Teamster scandals of the 1950s had given the U.S. Department of Labor new laws to police unions, so care had to be exercised in putting down the opposition. Nonetheless, the counterinsurgency ran the gamut from petty harassment to bully-boy tactics.

In the United Mine Workers *Journal,* for instance, Jock Yablonski suddenly became anathema. The official publication of the union came out every two weeks and was sent to all members, but suddenly the *Journal* ceased mentioning Yablonski's name except in a listing of executive board members, and references to the greatness of President Boyle increased geometrically. Yablonski went to court to gain the right to space in the *Journal,* but the delay in the legal action cost him five important issues in which he was a nonperson.

Then Boyle ordered Yablonski removed as acting director of Labor's Non-Partisan League, claiming that Yablonski was unable to do his job. He won a court fight against that, too. To conduct his campaign, Yablonski needed the mailing lists of union members. The lists were refused. Yablonski sued again and won the right to the lists, only to run into a union-arranged delay over using bulk-postage meters.

Yablonski claimed that he spent only $60,000 on his six-month campaign, while, he noted, the union leadership had millions at its disposal. But Yablonski had a tireless ally in his attorney, the gutsy and liberal Washington lawyer Joseph L. Rauh, Jr. A lanky, unflappable, gray-haired man who had

begun his career in the 1930s as a law clerk to Justices Frank-
furter and Cardozo. Rauh took on Yablonski's cause with the
kind of dedication he later put into the successful fight against
President Nixon's nomination of G. Harrold Carswell to the
Supreme Court. When the first obstructive reactions started
filtering out of 900 Fifteenth Street, Rauh, at his office a few
blocks away, began mounting Yablonski's massive legal assault
on the union hierarchy.

Although the union election was not until December 8, the
union's rules provided that, to get on the ballot, candidates had
to obtain the nominations of fifty of the union's thirteen hundred locals. The nomination period was between July 9 and
August 9. Before the Boyle-run convention of 1964, the union
constitution required only five union-local nominations to get
a spot on the ballot. In effect, then, there were two election
campaigns in 1969—one for the nomination and the bitter four-
month battle for the presidency.

Yablonski's initial drive hardly got off the ground when he
ran into barriers, some of them physical. He claimed that some
local-union meetings were broken up by paid goons hired to
prevent him from obtaining nominations. Smaller locals that
might have been pro-Yablonski were suddenly absorbed into
larger, pro-Boyle locals. Yablonski supporters found that nominating meetings had already taken place when they showed up
to vote. Several locals in the anthracite region of northeastern
Pennsylvania provided notice of their nominating meeting by
advertising in the classified section of a newspaper—without
describing the office to be voted upon. One local in Virginia
nominated Yablonski, heard from a district officer, then held
another vote nominating Boyle. And there were threats, intimi-
dations, and visits to Yablonski supporters by burly loyalists of
President Boyle.

Convinced that Yablonski would not even get on the ballot
for the December election, attorney Rauh began peppering
President Nixon's Secretary of Labor, George P. Shultz, with
complaints, pleas for investigations, data charging scores of

violations of the Landrum-Griffin Act. That law had been
passed ten years earlier and was designed to protect rank-and-
file members from tyrannical union bosses, but the power it gave
the Department of Labor had never really been tested. Shultz
might have invoked his power to have the government intervene
in the election, but he chose to exercise an option not to. His
argument was that Yablonski first had to exercise his own internal remedies within the union.

While all this was being fought over by the lawyers for both
sides, Boyle made some internal moves of his own. John L.
Lewis died on June 11, 1969, and his trusteeship on the UMW
Welfare and Retirement Fund thereby became vacant. Twelve
days later, at a meeting of the UMW international executive
board, Boyle moved to have himself named to the vacancy.
Yablonski attended the meeting, but abstained from voting.
Boyle became one of three trustees of the Fund—there was also
an industry representative and a neutral trustee. The latter, an
aged Lewis disciple named Josephine Roche, was ill, and Boyle
claimed that he was authorized to cast her Fund vote by proxy.
With an eye on the huge bloc of pensioned miners' votes, Boyle
rammed through a $35-a-month increase in union pensions. The
action was financially questionable, but the pensioned soft-coal
miners would now get $150 a month, giving them good reason
to vote overwhelmingly for President Boyle.

Boyle moved on another front that would guarantee his
reelection. About five hundred union employees became coal-
dust committeemen, checkers, and organizers, when actually
they were campaigning full time for the Boyle slate. (At least
three middle-level union officials were later convicted of illegally
diverting expenses to Boyle's campaign chest.)

Yablonski always feared that physical violence might be
perpetrated on himself, which was why he would not make any
appearances in District 19, in Tennessee and eastern Kentucky.
Just a month after he announced his candidacy, he was campaigning in Springfield, Illinois, when a man came up behind
him and knocked him unconscious. Yablonski said that it was

a karate chop; the Department of Labor said the assailant was never found; the FBI said that it was a punch on the chin and that the assailant was not paid to deliver the blow. But whatever the circumstances, Yablonski supporters charged that no serious investigation of the incident was made while Yablonski was alive.

Despite the obstacles, Yablonski won the required fifty nominations and then some. He was on the ballot. By Labor Day, the campaign for the UMW presidency was on. Boyle's forces hired a public-relations firm that had specialized in political campaigns. The incumbent president, noting that the union had "tremendous catching up to do," began making promises; he would fight for a $50-a-day base pay for miners, an increase in the royalty paid by coal operators, $200-a-month retirement pensions, and a commission to look into the possibility of the election of district officers. To all this, Yablonski sneered: "It is indicative of Mr. Boyle's imagination that it took three months and the counsel of a high-priced political adviser before he realized I had a good idea."

Through the coal fields, Boyle's supporters mined every trace of a skeleton in Jock Yablonski's past. Handbills charging Yablonski with "conflict of interest" were circulated by the thousand. They charged that Yablonski's family had received valuable water rights from coal companies because of Yablonski's prominence in the union's District 5. They accused Yablonski of "political shakedown," of holding huge amounts of stock in a Pennsylvania race track. Whisper campaigns dredged up Yablonski's conviction, nearly forty years earlier during the Depression, for breaking into a vending machine. They portrayed him as a "child deserter" because of his first marriage many years before. He was labeled a scab and a strikebreaker and "Holy Joe." There were hints that he had made a fortune off the backs of mine workers. When he offered to debate Boyle on a West Virginia television station, Boyle refused.

Yablonski continued to press the Department of Labor to intervene, and police the election. There was going to be fraud,

intimidation of voters, and violence, he warned. Secretary
Shultz steadfastly refused. Attorney Rauh churned out reams
of what he considered evidence for government intervention to
guarantee a fair election, but Shultz said it was "long-standing
policy" not to investigate labor elections before the balloting.*

Nonetheless, the Labor Department did drop what it considered a bombshell less than two weeks before the union election.
After an eight-month investigation, the department released a
summary of an audit of one aspect of the UMW's financial
affairs. It said that the three top union officials—Boyle, Vice
President George Titler, and Secretary-Treasurer John Owens
—and their relatives received nearly $400,000 in salaries and
expenses in 1967. It said that in 1960, a fund then totaling $850,-
000 was set up by the union to finance retirement at full salary
for the three top officers. The fund had grown to $1.5 million
but had never been adequately disclosed in financial reports to
the government. In Boyle's case alone, retirement at full salary
would mean $50,000 a year, compared with $1800 a year for the
coal miner lucky enough to qualify for a pension.

The Department of Labor audit also discovered loose re-
porting of union expenses. Some officials claimed hotel expenses
when they were at home, one official claimed twenty dollars a
day every day he was on vacation, and for Secretary-Treasurer
Owens there was an $11,500-a-year outlay for a Washington
hotel suite.

The Department of Labor turned the report over to the
Internal Revenue Service for "possible criminal prosecution."
Boyle charged that the audit was "a smear job and open union
busting." But it was hardly the bombshell its government au-

* In an interview with this writer in May 1973, William J. Usery, who was
Assistant Secretary of Labor at the time of the 1969 election, conceded that the
department could have investigated. Usery added: "But that's all we could do.
We had no way to go. The law is pretty specific. Unions have the right, and
it's in the law, to exhaust all their internal remedies before we could go into
court or before we could get any relief. . . . Now any time that you play football,
try to quarterback a football game on Monday that was played last Saturday,
maybe you could call a play a little early or a little different or some other way.
But basically I think we were right in our judgment as to what we did there."

thors figured it would be. Much of it had been public record before. Yablonski said that it substantiated his own charges of union nepotism and cronyism, but he added that it seemed only to have skimmed the surface of the UMW's financial affairs. His basic demand—Department of Labor intervention to prevent fraud at the polls—went unheeded.

Only a month before the election, Yablonski asked a federal court to help guarantee fair voting. At the hearings, Boyle's seventy-six-year-old secretary-treasurer and running-mate, John Owens, testified that fifty thousand extra ballots were printed for use in the election. His explanation: "Because sometimes the ballots don't reach the locals" in time for the election. The judge hearing the case said that the court was powerless to do anything, and he commented that the union officials "pay attention to the [union] constitution when they want to and don't when they don't."

In a final appeal to Secretary Shultz a week before the December 8 election, Joseph Rauh warned:

"The failure of the Department of Labor to take strong measures to insure a fair election may well bring in its train ugly violence in the mines. There is a deep hatred among the coal miners of the incumbent leadership of the UMWA. If that hatred is fanned by a belief that the election was stolen from the rightful winner by the incumbent leadership, the cost in violence, strikes, and slowdowns may be greater than you or anyone thinks."

On the day of the balloting, Yablonski's camp sent hundreds of observers to the polling places, but they couldn't be everywhere, and they stayed away entirely from the vehemently anti-Yablonski District 19 in Tennessee and Kentucky. Nonetheless they were able to document violations: voters marking ballots in full view of Boyle tellers, locals that received more ballots than they had members, observers unable to find out where the balloting was being conducted. One local reported its tally as fifty-nine for Boyle, one for Yablonski; its membership list contained fifty-seven names. In Pikesville, Kentucky, the Commit-

tee for the Re-Election of Our International Officers operated
out of the district headquarters, with the committee chairman
receiving a salary of $11,130 as district representative. Elderly
miners—once their loyalty to Boyle was determined—were
given free transportation to the polls. Boyle campaign literature
was liberally sprinkled around the voting area. The tabulation
in District 19 alone—Boyle 3275, Yablonski 87—was not only
suspiciously lopsided but was available hours before the official
end of the balloting.

In view of the inherent advantages of an incumbent slate,
the outcome of the UMW election was hardly surprising. The
official figures, announced long after midnight by Boyle, showed
Boyle with 81,056 votes, Yablonski with 45,872. As expected,
Boyle ran up a big margin among the pensioned miners, gaining
something like 80 percent of their vote. Among working miners,
the margin was closer to a fifty-fifty split.

But Yablonski's fight wasn't over. Three days after the election, he informed the Department of Labor and Boyle that he
wanted the ballots impounded. He accused Boyle of "outright
bribery and intimidation," and he said that sixty thousand members had been permitted to vote through seven hundred illegally
constituted local unions—so-called "bogus" locals made up of
fewer than ten active miners. Yablonski said that Boyle would
"stop at nothing to maintain his fiefdom."

At four o'clock in the morning on December 14, Yablonski
got a call at his home. A wire service wanted to know if it was
true that he had conceded the election to Boyle. That night in
West Virginia, Yablonski told a crowd of supporters the union
had put out the story.

"They've planted stories coming out of everywhere!" he
sneered. "This was the most dishonest election that has ever
been held in the history of the united labor movement. We'll
never concede to that type of dishonesty as long as it exists.

"There may be some attempts at reprisals against some people in some sections of the country. There may be an attempt

to fire some people at work. Well, I want to say this to the coal operators and I want to say this to Tony Boyle and all his stooges: You try it!

"We'll be happy to concede after we've had an election that's corruption-free. When the election is totally honest, monitored by people who will see to it that it is honest. If, then, the count would show that I was the loser, I'd be the first to congratulate the winner. As it has been conducted, the fight is going to go on, to bring about a union that's truly responsive to its membership. A union that is totally corruption-free. A union that's totally democratic. And that fight will go on!"

The next day, December 15, Yablonski was in Washington at Secretary Shultz's invitation for a conference at the Department of Labor. Yablonski had been asked to produce evidence supporting his charges of election violations. Yablonski, Joseph Rauh, and their supporters made clear that they would continue the battle, first through the United Mine Workers and then in the courts. On December 18, ten days after the election, Yablonski sent a formal letter to the union disputing the election returns, and he hurled this ironic challenge to the men who had counted the ballots:

"Tellers, stand up before it's too late. I, too, once submitted to the discipline of Tony Boyle. But I shall die an honest man because I finally rejected that discipline."

Thirteen days later, on December 31, 1969, at about one o'clock in the morning, three men crept into the bedrooms of Jock Yablonski, his wife Margaret, and their daughter Charlotte, and shot them to death.

The First Assistant

IN EARLY JANUARY 1970, a young man had a fight with his landlady in a Cleveland rooming house. His name was Aubran Martin; he had a southern accent and a criminal record going back to the age of fifteen. (He still looked around seventeen, but was actually twenty-one.) He was a common burglar and a tough kid despite his childish appearance, and so he fought with the landlady when she asked him to move a car that was blocking her driveway. Martin was recovering from too many beers the night before, and he threatened and cursed the woman. She called the police; Aubran Martin fought with them, too, and thereby wound up with a fifty-five-day jail sentence.

Not far away on the East Side of Cleveland, a twenty-six-year-old dark-haired fellow who know Martin also got in trouble with the law. This man's name was Claude Vealey, and like Martin, he had both a southern accent and a burglary record. Several months earlier, Vealey had threatened to kill his common-law wife, but she hadn't pressed charges. But a burglary rap got Vealey in trouble again. Accused of committing a burglary in Youngstown, Vealey failed to show up for his hearing, and a day or so after the three Yablonski bodies were found in Pennsylvania, Claude Vealey was back in jail in Ohio on the burglary charge.

An older man named Paul Gilly knew both these characters, but was seemingly more respectable than they. Southern-born like the rest, Gilly was a thirty-six-year-old house painter who also ran a cheap Cleveland diner called Dalton's Restaurant. Gilly dabbled in fencing stolen weapons and coins. He had managed not to run afoul of the law, but thanks to Aubran Martin and Claude Vealey, Gilly wound up in a Cleveland jail, too, that January of 1970.

And it didn't help any of them that a man named James Charles Phillips was in and out of Cleveland bars that winter. Phillips had a few things going against him: He wasn't very bright, he had a big mouth (also with a southern accent), and he was quite impressed with his performance with women. He took his mouth to saloons in East Cleveland, mainly to one known as the Family Tavern, and over countless beers he began hinting that he'd been involved in a big job in Pennsylvania. Other Appalachians living in Cleveland, some underworld characters, and some loose-talking women overheard Phillip's disjointed story.

By the third week of January, as FBI agents fanned out over the East, the South, and the Midwest, they kept hearing the name Phillips in the Cleveland area. The trail led to the Family Tavern, where Phillips was supposed to live, but he wasn't there. He had disappeared. The FBI men weren't worried; they knew that eventually he'd turn up. Besides, the lawmen already had some of the clues they needed—back in Yablonski's home in Clarksville.

The first tangible piece of evidence in the case, besides the twelve spent bullets, was the yellow notepad in Jock Yablonski's den. Scribbled on it was a license number, "CX457," followed by the word "Ohio," and after that two names, "Annette Gilly" and "Paul Gilly, house painter." The words were written in Jock Yablonski's hand, and it took no great investigative work to find out what they meant.

On December 18, 1969, Yablonski had had some unexpected visitors to his house. Two men—one of them heavy and dark-haired and the other thin and dark—showed up at his door, professing to be miners seeking jobs. Yablonski was immediately suspicious, but he told them to go to the United Mine Workers. When they left, he and his son Ken and a friend, Karl Kafton, who were in the house, decided to look for the pair's car.

They drove into the business area of Clarksville, about a mile or so from Yablonski's farmhouse. As they got to a telephone booth, they spotted the car—a 1965 maroon Chevy. They wrote down the license number, CX457 OHIO.

Later, at Yablonski's house, Karl Kafton called a friend at the motor vehicle bureau in Ohio, to check out the registration of the Chevy. He was told that it was listed under the name of Annette Gilly, in Cleveland. Kafton then called Cleveland's information operator, got the telephone number for the Gilly address, and dialed the number. A woman answered. Kafton, posing as a Pennsylvania state policeman, asked her some questions. She identified herself as Annette Gilly. She didn't seem alarmed when Kafton said the car might have been involved in an accident. Yablonski wrote down the woman's name and her husband's, and there the incident ended—until after the murders.

In Cleveland in the early weeks of January 1970, the FBI checked out Paul Gilly, but he seemed to be what he claimed to be—a house painter—and the only mark on his record was a nonsupport charge many years before. His wife Annette seemed to have no record, either. Her father was a man named Silous Huddleston who lived in LaFollette, Tennessee, an official of a pensioners' local union in the United Mine Workers, in the heart of District 19, where Yablonski had feared to campaign. And Paul Gilly's father was a retired coal miner. But those facts didn't fit the puzzle—yet.

Claude Vealey wasn't talking, and neither were Aubran Martin and Paul Gilly. James Charles Phillips seemed to be the key man. Phillips. Vealey. Martin. Gilly. Four names of four small-time criminals. Where did they fit together? Agents like Joseph Masterson, a dark-haired good-looking veteran of six years in the FBI Cleveland office, went over the records and questioned the suspects, but the big break didn't come until Phillips turned himself in.

Phillips had been staying with an uncle in hiding, but as word of the Yablonski murders began to saturate the news outlets, the uncle had second thoughts about harboring a potential murder defendant who could tell the authorities what they wanted to know. And Phillips himself had his eye on two things —a possible reward of $50,000 put up by the United Mine Workers, and the ever-present threat of Pennsylvania's death penalty.

So Phillips cracked and told Agent Masterson and others that there had been many trips to Pennsylvania, to Clarksville, to Yablonski's home. Phillips said that he had gone along with Claude Vealey and Paul Gilly. They were going to kill this guy named Yablonski, Phillips didn't know why. They had driven to Washington, D.C., and had made another trip to Scranton, Pennsylvania, but couldn't find the elusive Yablonski. Each time, he said, they were scared, and each time he went along they couldn't find him. It all covered a period of five months, but Phillips said he eventually had an argument with the other two and decided to drop out of it.

The FBI agents asked Claude Vealey about the trips he had made with Paul Gilly and Phillips, they mentioned little details about guns, cars, phone calls. Vealey became aware that the FBI men knew what they were talking about, and he became aware, too, that he might face a murder charge in Pennsylvania, with a chance to be sentenced to die in the electric chair.

It was too much for Vealey. Some ten days after the discovery of the Yablonski bodies, Vealey confessed that he had been involved in the murders. He named the other two men who had killed the Yablonskis with him—Paul Gilly, the seemingly respectable house painter, and Aubran Martin. On January 21, 1970, the FBI in Cleveland announced the arrest of Claude Vealey, Paul Gilly, and Aubran Martin. They were named as the killers of the three Yablonskis. They were held on federal charges of depriving a union member of his civil rights. And in Washington, Pennsylvania, they were charged with murder.

Sixteen days had now gone by since Ken Yablonski had uncovered the slaughter in the farmhouse, and the United Mine Workers and Tony Boyle were coming under increasing public pressure. Within the union, Yablonski's insurgent movement was picked up by his sons, both lawyers. They began forming an organization known as Miners for Democracy, and plunged into legal battles at both the district and international levels of the union. While Chip Yablonski and Joseph Rauh continued the court fight to overturn the election, Louis Antal, a short, cocky veteran of the western Pennsylvania coal fields, began to challenge the Tony Boyle power structure in Jock Yablonski's old District 5. Another district election was coming up there in December 1970, and Antal trained his sights on Yablonski's successor, a Boyle loyalist.

In Washington, Congressman Ken Hechler, the West Virginia Democrat who had been Yablonski's ally, put the pressure on the Department of Labor to investigate the election and the union. Hechler, along with Ralph Nader, had been a leading advocate of the 1969 Coal Mine Health and Safety Act, which, for the first time in nearly twenty years, gave the government new weapons to protect coal miners' working conditions. The Senate Labor Subcommittee, headed by New Jersey Democrat Harrison Williams, stepped up the pace of hearings into the affairs of the United Mine Workers, giving the Miners for Democracy a forum to attack the Boyle leadership. And the Department of Justice made plans to revive its long-dormant suit to break up the trusteeships under which Boyle held power over the union's districts.

Boyle's consistent reaction to the murder of the Yablonskis was to deplore them, and to deny any connection between them and the union. The union put up a $50,000 reward for information leading to the conviction of the killers, and the union also said it welcomed government investigators. They descended on

the union in droves, from the FBI, the Department of Labor
and the Department of Justice.

But despite the official mourning, bitterness toward Yablonski persisted in the union hierarchy. In February 1970, George
Titler, Boyle's crusty seventy-six-year-old vice president, gave
an unusual two-hour interview to a reporter in Charleston, West
Virginia, where Titler was hospitalized with spinal arthritis. He
called Yablonski a notorious thief, said he was "so goddam
crooked he could hide behind a corkscrew," and ventured the
opinion that his murder was probably ordered by persons he
had swindled. Said Titler: "Joe Yablonski was the crookedest
bastard we ever had. I'll say that even though he's dead. He stole
more votes in the years he was in the UMW. . . .

"All this talk to make him a martyr is just a lot of hogwash.
There were millions and millions of dollars behind Joe Yablonski, trying to destroy the UMW. He was hired for that very
purpose."

When Titler was asked why the union would retain someone
so crooked, he said that headquarters in Washington had no
choice, because Yablonski had been elected by the membership.
"You don't know that foreign element of coal miners from
Russia and Yugoslavia and the like up there in Pennsylvania.
I don't mean there's anything wrong with being foreign, but
they stick together and stick behind their man. It's not like
down in the Kentucky fields or some place where everybody's
Anglo-Saxon."

A few days after Titler's statement, Tony Boyle called a
press conference in Pittsburgh, the heart of District 5, for his
first full-scale meeting with news reporters since the murders.
He was coming under increasing attack in the press, and he
wanted to set the record straight in Jock Yablonski's backyard.

Boyle announced that he was setting up a fact-finding commission to look into the Yablonski murders. Boyle invited everyone, including Yablonski's family and union supporters, to
come forth with any information. Yablonski's sons ridiculed the

commission as "Tony Boyle's show trial," and refused to be a part of it. Several weeks later, the commission, manned by four Boyle appointees, did hold a hearing in Pittsburgh, supposedly the first of many. Lengthy testimony attacking Yablonski's background was presented, none of it under oath, and after two days the Boyle commission closed shop. It never held another meeting.

While Boyle was in Pittsburgh, he went on television to talk about his much maligned union. When he was asked about George Titler's hospital-bed statements, Boyle hinted that Titler may have spoken under sedation.

Did Boyle disagree with Titler?

"No," said Boyle, "I don't disagree with it in this respect: that we disagree in toto with the amount of money that they [the Yablonski supporters] say they spent [in the election campaign]. . . . For someone to say that he only spent sixty thousand dollars, that's an insult to the intelligence of anyone that ever ran for office, you know, because a closer figure to that would be, instead of sixty thousand dollars, six hundred thousand dollars would be a closer figure in my judgment."

(In sworn testimony before a Senate subcommittee several weeks earlier, Chip Yablonski had said that his father's campaign cost $60,000.)

Boyle was asked where Yablonski might get that kind of money.

"I wouldn't know where he got it," he said, "but you take that campaign that was put on. The plush campaign that was put on. They make no denials of the fact that they put on a plush campaign, and headquarters all over the country. It would cost considerable money. I don't know how much it would cost."

Sounding like the ailing George Titler, Boyle charged that "outsiders had a great influence on Joe Yablonski . . . in trying to take over the operation of this union." However, Boyle would not name the outsiders, except to describe them as "doctors, lawyers, and phony politicians. None of them ever worked in a coal mine or belonged to this union."

Finally, Boyle accused Yablonski of nepotism, and said he was sure that coal miners were not involved "in this tragic thing that happened. . . . I don't know why they would kill Joe Yablonski."

In Washington, Boyle and the United Mine Workers began a counterattack against the most vehement assault on a labor union since the days of James R. Hoffa and the Teamsters. Boyle blasted the "totalitarian liberal establishment" for conducting a "journalistic lynching bee." He charged that it was a prelude to an attack on all labor. He denied categorically that the UMW had had any contact whatsoever with the three alleged Yablonski triggermen. He denied charges of intimidation during the union election. He went before the National Press Club, raised his right hand, with its missing little finger, and swore to Almighty God that he was telling the truth. And with the UMW's help, a publication known as *American Labor* published a lengthy diatribe against Jock Yablonski. "Equal time for Tony Boyle," the publication screamed, but the only source it could quote was the right-wing labor columnist Victor Riesel, whose fulminations had long since been ignored by the bulk of organized labor.

But not to be ignored were the demands for an investigation of the UMW and the urgings for action to bring about a new election. The Department of Labor was caught in the middle: Chip Yablonski and Joseph Rauh kept accusing the department of not moving fast enough, and Boyle's forces were annoyed when the department showed signs of going into court. The net effect of the swirl of charges was to cloud the investigation of the Yablonski murders. In the coal fields, the miners who had twice had to choose sides in the previous seven months now had to take a stand again.

The contempt for Yablonski from the hierarchy of the United Mine Workers reverberated in Washington County, Pennsylvania, where Yablonski had legions of enemies and friends. When the three accused triggermen were arrested in Cleveland, there was both relief and disappointment on the victim's home ground. The relief came from followers of Tony Boyle, from small-time politicians, and from union men who believed everything their leaders told them. "Yablonski was probably killed by somebody he swindled," was the refrain that echoed among workers in coal, steel, and autos. There was speculation that the Mafia might be behind the killings, and there were predictions that the indictments of Vealey, Martin, and Gilly would mark the end of the case. The local politicians, with their eyes on the 1971 elections, predicted three quick trials in Pennsylvania and then, with a difficult, controversial case out of the way, back to politics as usual.

Dissappointment over the progress of the murder investigation came from Yablonski's two sons. Ken Yablonski, practicing law in Washington County, knew the union territory well from having represented miners in compensation claims. He agonized over the thought that this might be the conclusion of the murder case, but he vowed never to rest until those who had ordered the killings were caught. And his brother Chip, practicing law in Washington, D.C., was equally determined to see that the case went forward. Chip saw the workings of the international union first hand, and he was not going to let his father's movement die in the cemetery at Washington, Pennsylvania.

But early in 1970, the prospect of finding out and proving who wanted Yablonski killed seemed bleak. Paul Gilly and Aubran Martin weren't talking, and Claude Vealey's confession gave little clue to higher-ups. Miners in the union's Appalachian districts rallied to the defense of Tony Boyle's leadership, and much of the rest of organized labor remained silent. In Washington County, the resources of the local prosecutors were taxed beyond their ability to handle a full-scale investigation, and soon rivalries, jealousies, and petty political disputes were arising from among the various levels of government involved in the investigation. From Cleveland, where a government attorney had his eye on a judgeship, to Washington, Pennsylvania, where new clashes over the UMW leadership divided men's loyalties, the Yablonski murder case was about to bog down in the political quicksand of everyday law enforcement. But this was not an everyday case.

Enter one man who turned the case around.

Late on an afternoon in February 1970, the telephone rang in the office of the district attorney of Philadelphia. A deputy to the Pennsylvania attorney general was calling from Harrisburg, the state capital. He spoke to Philadelphia's first assistant district attorney, Richard Aurel Sprague. Their conversation was brief: Would Sprague be interested in prosecuting a murder case in southwestern Pennsylvania? The Yablonski murder case—three hundred miles from where Sprague was then sitting. All Sprague knew about the case was what he had read in the papers, but he said Yes, he would be interested.

Sprague appeared to be an unlikely-seeming prosecutor. He was of medium height, about five feet seven, and, at forty-six, had the beginnings of a potbelly and double chins. He had a severe face that seldom smiled and protruding brown eyes that distracted attention from the rest of him. Everything about him seemed conventional: he had short dark hair with no sideburns, always wore conservative blue or gray business suits with nondescript ties, and, each business day, affixed a tie clip bearing the seal of the City of Philadelphia. His hands were small and his handshake was clammy, and at first glance he seemed the squarest of men, not the sort who would be comfortable in the role of star prosecutor.

But Sprague only seemed ordinary. In the courtroom this slight, somewhat shy man metamorphosed into a giant. The bulging eyes that could distract in conversation would fix on a testifying defendant or a shyster lawyer, producing a withering effect on one who would waver from the straight and narrow of the courtroom. His booming bass voice, tinged with a Philadelphia accent, had guided the prosecution of sixty-five accused murderers in his ten years as first assistant, and Sprague had won sixty-four first-degree convictions and one second-degree verdict.

In the courtroom, his behavior was unorthodox, even bizarre. While other lawyers scribbled volumes on their yellow pads during the progress of a case, Sprague never took a note. He never had a yellow notebook before him, but instead would watch the defendant for telltale signs or fix his eyes on the jury to see which way the case was going. Imprinting every word of testimony on his retentive brain, he could rise up and deliver a two-hour summation to a jury without a note or a break in a sentence. He seldom consulted lawbooks or transcripts of testimony. Sprague remembered every case he ever tried—and learned from each. He had learned the folly of overconfidence, as when he contemptuously tossed a bit of clinching evidence—a cigarette lighter—to a jury, which then found the defendant not guilty. The courtroom, he had learned early in his career, was not a place for such displays.

Though his record as first assistant was unblemished in capital cases, Richard Sprague was a man of superstitions and regular habits. Whenever a jury retired to deliberate in one of his cases, he would never leave the courthouse until the jury returned or was locked up overnight. And during jury deliberations, he ate only one dish—a chocolate malted. Inside, his system churned, but outwardly he appeared cool. Yet any time someone asked him how he thought a case might turn out, Sprague would smile, decline to answer, and knock three times on the nearest wood.

A measure of his effectiveness in the Philadelphia district attorney's office was that he was kept on through several changes of administration. The first assistant was the chief executive officer in an office with one hundred fifty attorneys, and for more than a decade Sprague was the man who ran the everyday affairs of the prosecution of cases in the nation's fourth largest city. By the time of the Yablonski murder case, Sprague had built a reputation as the leading prosecutor in Pennsylvania. Now, on top of his duties as first assistant, he accepted the role of special prosecutor for the Commonwealth of Pennsylvania. Sprague's reasons, like the man, were complex.

First, it was almost unheard of in Pennsylvania for one district attorney to request the intervention of another. The D.A. in Washington County, overwhelmed by the complexities and political implications of the Yablonski murders, had asked Harrisburg for help, and the attorney general, a Republican, had asked the top prosecutor in Pennsylvania, a Democrat, to take the job. For Sprague, it was a feather in his cap, and that was a consideration.

Then, too, it was a new kind of case for Sprague. In his trial work going back to 1958, he had run a grisly gamut of killers. They ranged from impulsive, youthful murderers (one was a fourteen-year-old boy whose own father had died in the electric chair) to raging psychotics (one, a hulking monster named Birdman Phelan, had done in two persons, for hire, and threatened to murder Sprague himself). Sprague had sent to life in prison a man whose victim's body was never found, and he had gained a conviction against a man involved in the murders of two Teamsters, on what many lawyers considered insufficient evidence.

Although the Yablonski case also involved a union, it was a new turn in the road for Sprague. There were three suspects in custody in Cleveland, and FBI agents were ranging over the coal fields looking for more, so the case wouldn't end with one or two trials. Obviously, Sprague reasoned, it would be an ongoing investigation, perhaps lasting several years, and he would have a chance to show that rival political agencies—the Justice Department, the FBI, the state police, and local authorities— could work together.

The brutality of the case also promised to provide Sprague a forum for his unshaken belief that Pennsylvania must carry out its death penalty, unused in the state since 1962. Sprague had sent seventeen men to death row, but only one of them, the killer of a storekeeper, had gone to the electric chair. (That case had its own bizarre side, since the killer was found guilty twice and sentenced to the chair twice. Between the trials, Pennsylvania's Supreme Court had laid down rules for separate jury deliberations on verdict and penalty, and Sprague could claim a hand in that.)

The Yablonski case, Sprague realized, was unlike anything else in his experience. It would take him far from Philadelphia, to the soft-coal fields, and for an urban prosecutor that was an attraction, too. In assuming the role of special prosecutor in the Yablonski murders, Sprague was entering a quagmire whose depths he would plumb for more than four years. He was entering the kingdom of coal, where violent death is a way of life.

In February 1970, one of Sprague's first moves was to fly to Cleveland, where a federal grand jury was questioning dozens of officials of the United Mine Workers, all of whom swore they knew nothing about the Yablonski murders. Claude Vealey wanted to see the new prosecutor in the case. He felt that his confession entitled him to something: if not the reward money, then a deal that he would not be sentenced to the electric chair if he went back to Pennsylvania to stand trial. Sprague agreed to see him.

The meeting took place in the federal courthouse in Cleveland. It was still cold outside and the windows were shut tight, emphasizing the slight odor that emanated from Claude Vealey, who was not bathing regularly in the jailhouse in Cleveland.

"Vealey offered to testify fully in Pennsylvania," Sprague recalls, "if I would give him a guarantee that I would not ask for the electric chair. He was scared to death of that possibility. I refused. And I remember the FBI agents, the U.S. attorney—everybody in the room!—they all looked at me as if I was crazy. And I said, 'No, I'm not going to make a deal with you.'

"For a very good reason: this was the beginning of the case, not the end, as far as I was concerned. My own standing as a prosecutor was going to be tested an awful lot. If they think right off the bat, 'Here's some namby-pamby prosecutor we can make deals with,' my chances of working the case back go down proportionately. I was not anxious for quick convictions at that point.

"I looked straight at Vealey and said, 'Boy, you got no deal.' I wasn't going to let any of the participants blackjack me into any agreement I didn't want to make.

"Remember this, too: I was setting out to work with federal agents, local officers, and state police. I had to make sure all competing and conflicting agencies knew there was one guy in total command—me."

Vealey was taken back to his jail cell in Cleveland, where he decided to fight against extradition to Pennsylvania. Which was fine with Sprague, because a long delay would give the investigators more time to trace the source of the Yablonski murders.

Sprague then arranged another sort of meeting—with Jock Yablonski's two sons, Ken and Chip. Both were lawyers, and both were bitter about every lawyer from Ralph Nader to the Justice Department. Nader had encouraged their father to run against Tony Boyle and then, in their view, he had withdrawn from the campaign, leaving their father out on a limb in the six-month union election campaign. Their father had complained to the government about crookedness and potential violence, but the government had done nothing. Now, they thought, three punks were under arrest, people were saying the case was solved, and the Yablonskis were being asked to trust some lawyer from Philadelphia.

Ken and Chip flew to Philadelphia to meet with the special prosecutor. They gathered in Sprague's small, cluttered fifth-floor office in Philadelphia's City Hall. They began warily on a weekend and before the talks were over, they had held two ten-hour sessions. Sprague asked many questions, listened for long periods, and as was his custom, didn't take one note.

They talked about Jock Yablonski, what kind of man he was, why he had decided to buck the UMW leadership of Tony Boyle. They talked about why Yablonski had turned his back on forty years of loyal service to the union leadership, about what the union meant to coal miners, and about his determination to overturn the union establishment even though Boyle had won the election. And Ken and Chip Yablonski made clear to Sprague that despite what others might say, *they* were convinced that the union leadership had played a role in silencing Jock Yablonski.

The Yablonski sons gave Sprague some insight into the area of southwestern Pennsylvania, where the murder trials would begin. Sprague had never tried a case there before, and he knew little about the local politics or how the union figured in people's everyday lives. The special prosecutor absorbed it all; and he did more. A participant in the meetings remembers:

"Dick Sprague did something few people would have the guts to do. But it was necessary. He took Claude Vealey's statement—twenty-one typewritten pages—and he read it aloud to Chip and Ken Yablonski, one sentence at a time. It hadn't been made public yet. He read it word for word. And then he would ask the two boys questions, quite specific questions, in some cases to see if it rang a bell in their memory, to see if Vealey's recollection of the inside of the house was correct.

"It was a very hard thing for Sprague to do. This was just a few weeks after the bodies were discovered—but he did it absolutely without showing emotion. You knew, though, that there was a great deal of emotion behind it, because Ken and Chip had never heard a thorough description, from the mouth of one of the murderers, of what happened in the house the night their parents and sister were slaughtered.

"Dick read every gory detail, including their father's final gurgle that was overheard by Vealey, and Mrs. Yablonski's screaming, and Charlotte getting two bullets point blank in the head."

Ken and Chip tried hard not to weep; but of course they both did at one point or another. And Sprague had to steel them for what lay ahead—an arduous investigation, three or four years of hearing that story repeated in courtrooms, the time-consuming pursuit of the instigators of the murders.

"I am not in this for the publicity," Sprague told the Yablonskis. "I am not running for any office. We are going to unlock this entire case, get back to the beginning and get everybody who was involved in it."

When the long sessions in Sprague's office were over that weekend, Ken and Chip Yablonski were convinced that the right man had been chosen to prosecute the murderers. And Richard Sprague, a man who doesn't draw conclusions easily, was sure of this: The United Mine Workers union was behind the murder of Jock Yablonski. Now all he had to do was prove it.

Sprague began with the notepad that had been found in Yablonski's desk. What interested him most was the name "Annette Gilly." Why had the killers found it necessary to call Annette Gilly, as Vealey's confession related? Sprague ordered telephone records collected, and in Scranton, Pennsylvania, he found a record of two calls from a gasoline station to Annette's house in Cleveland.

Annette Gilly told the grand jury in Cleveland, when her husband was in custody, that she knew nothing about the murders. So did her father, Silous Huddleston, when he was summoned from his home in LaFollette, Tennessee. More records began turning up—of motel meetings Huddleston's kin were having with a union representative in Tennessee. Some of the meetings were in motels only six miles from the union man's home. Was the union passing on money to keep Huddleston quiet? Sprague played a hunch. In February 1970 he ordered Annette Gilly and Silous Huddleston arrested on federal conspiracy charges in Cleveland. Now five suspects were in the net.

There was still no direct connection between the union and the murders. But an auditor in Washington, D.C., came upon two documents that rang bells in Sprague's mind.

The Department of Labor had been examining the United Mine Workers' books, seeking evidence for a court argument that the 1969 union election should be nullified and rerun. President Boyle and his associates turned over every scrap of paper to the government investigators. He was starting a new term as the union's leader and he had nothing to fear.

Out of thousands of pieces of paper, accounting for millions of dollars spent by the union in 1969, the government auditor found two short letters to Tony Boyle signed by an international board member of the union, Albert Pass. He ran the union's District 19, in eastern Kentucky and Tennessee. The two letters, dated in late September 1969, seemed like routine requests for money for District 19. Each letter asked for $10,000. A trace of the money showed that it filtered down from union headquarters in Washington, through the union-owned National Bank of Washington, to the headquarters of District 19 in Middlesboro, Kentucky, through the hands of union field representatives there, and thence by check to twenty-three pensioned miners. There was a total of forty-six checks—each retired miner got two, and each signed the check with his signature or an X. The retired miners, questioned by the federal grand jury in Cleveland, told the same story of having received the money for part-time organizing work for the union. And all the way up the line to Washington, everyone swore that the old men constituted a "Research and Information Committee" that had been formed at the union's international convention of 1968.

Nonsense, said Sprague.

"That," he said, "is the murder fund set up by the union to kill Jock Yablonski in 1969."

Was it possible that the union's own files contained evidence of a murder payoff?

"Sure," said Sprague. "What's a better way to conceal a murder fund than to have it right out in the open? If somebody opened his wallet and said, 'Here's twenty thousand dollars, get rid of Jock Yablonski,' it would be hard to conceal that amount of personal funds—what with bank records, expense vouchers, credit cards, all the little tracks your own money leaves these days.

"But in a union treasury of ninety million dollars or so, who would ever think that a twenty-thousand-dollar expenditure was anything but legitimate?"

What about the twenty-three elderly miners, who swore that they got the checks for their own use?

"They're lying," Sprague said. "They may not know what the money was used for, but they kicked that money back as soon as they got it, and it was covered up and passed on to the killers."

How could twenty-three men be made to lie without a break in their ranks?

"Fear," said Sprague. "They fear the union. They fear for their families. They fear for their hospital and pension cards. They've been *told,* ordered to lie because Albert Pass runs District Nineteen like Tony Boyle runs the international union. They will lie as long as they're afraid, but some day they're gonna tell the truth—and we'll be ready for them."

The letters to Boyle and the records of the checks to the miners went into the growing file with hundreds of other documents, while Sprague began putting his legal game plan in motion. The Yablonski case was nearly a year old now, but the trail of the killers and their superiors was growing warmer. The prosecutor began pushing the lowest pawns; it was time to begin extraditing the five suspects from Ohio to Pennsylvania.

Claude Vealey, the confessed killer, was first. He was fighting extradition because Sprague still wouldn't make a deal with him, but one of Sprague's aides used a legal device to get him to Pennsylvania. The aide arranged for a clerk to telephone Sprague's office collect when word of Vealey's appeal came down from the Ohio Supreme Court. (Vealey's lawyers could have done the same thing, but didn't.) Near the end of a court day in December 1970, the Ohio clerk called Philadelphia collect. The state's Supreme Court had turned down Vealey's appeal against extradition, and the decision would be announced the next morning. Before Vealey's lawyers could get the word, and possibly decide to go into the federal courts, Sprague sent a squad of deputy sheriffs from Washington County to Cleveland. That night, armed with the required documents, they put Vealey in a automobile and drove him out of Ohio along the route that he had followed a year before as a killer. In Washington County, he was placed in a local jail to await a court appearance, and soon after came Aubran Martin, Paul Gilly, Annette Gilly, and Silous Huddleston. Sprague ordered each of them put in different jails, so that they couldn't talk to each other, and each was indicted for murder. The scene now shifted to the Washington County Courthouse.

For his opening act in June 1971, Sprague led with Claude Vealey's plea of guilty. The prisoner was conviced that he was not going to get any deals from Sprague, and he would take his chances on leniency in return for his cooperation. Twenty-seven-year-old Vealey sat in the big, dark Courtroom Number One. He wore an open shirt and casual trousers as he listened to an FBI agent impassively read the statement taken when Vealey was arrested a year and a half earlier. The confession told of seven automobile trips in pursuit of Yablonski, starting in the summer of 1969. At several points, Vealey made reference to a "man named Tony," whom, he said, Gilly had occasion to call during their trips. "Tony" was not further identified in the statement.

Vealey's description of the murder scene itself was the most chilling part of the statement. He told how simple it was for him, Aubran Martin, and Paul Gilly to remove the door of the Yablonski farmhouse, and how the three intruders removed their own shoes before going inside.

"In the living room," said Vealey, "I took the M-one carbine from Paul [Gilly]. Buddy [Martin] had the thirty-eight chrome-plated revolver, and proceeded up the stairway, which is circular. At the top of the stairway there is a bedroom directly in front of this. I thought this was the bedroom of the daughter but it was empty. There is a short hallway to the right that we walked down and at the end of the hallway were two doors.

"The door on the left was open and led into Mr. and Mrs. Yablonski's bedroom. The door on the right was closed and led into the daughter's bedroom. I stood at Joseph Yablonski's bedroom door with the carbine; Paul Gilly was standing behind me. Buddy and I were to shoot simultaneously.

"Buddy opened the door to the bedroom and fired two shots into Charlotte Yablonski who was lying in bed. I aimed the carbine at the Yablonskis, who had awakened. Mrs. Yablonski laid in bed and was screaming, and Mr. Yablonski was getting up. I tried to fire the carbine and it did not work. I thought the safety was on, pushed a button, but this was the magazine release and it fell to the floor.

"Paul Gilly took the weapon from me, picked up the clip from the floor, put it back in the weapon, fired one time at the Yablonskis, and tried to fire again but the gun jammed. Buddy Martin came over, stepped just inside the door and fired four times, emptying his gun at the Yablonskis. After Buddy fired, the woman made no further sounds, and I could hear Yablonski gurgling.

"I took the weapon from Buddy, the thirty-eight-caliber revolver, fully loaded it again, walked into the Yablonski bedroom, and stood at the foot of the bed near the dresser and fired two shots at Joseph Yablonski. When I fired, Yablonski had fallen to a sitting position on the floor.

"Buddy came into the room and took some paper money, which was contained in a money clip, off the dresser located at the foot of the bed. I later learned that there was two hundred forty dollars contained in this money clip, which we split three ways. I then walked into the daughter's room, saw that she was not moving in her bed, checked her dresser for any money and found none, and returned to where Buddy and Paul were."

Vealey said that they disposed of the two guns in the Monongahela River, then drove back to Cleveland, arriving there about eight hours later, late on the morning of December 31. They had some beers in a Cleveland bar, received payoff money from

Gilly—$1700 each, minus $750 which Gilly had spent for Vea-ley's earlier bail bond—and Vealey bought a 1963 Oldsmobile with $500 of his night's income.

After his guilty plea, Claude Vealey's sentence was held in abeyance; his cooperation was needed in future trials. Prosecutor Sprague now began preparing for the case of Aubran Martin, which would take place in Sprague's favorite arena—before a jury in a courtroom.

4

"Very Few Souls Are Saved After Twenty Minutes"

WASHINGTON, PENNSYLVANIA, is not exactly sleepy, but not much ever happens there, either. If its courts have three murder cases going simultaneously, that's considered a busy season. In southwestern Pennsylvania it is known as "Little Washington," in case anyone should confuse it with that other Washington on the Potomac. One finds Little Washington by driving about forty minutes southwest of Pittsburgh, and just over the horizon is the West Virginia border.

Special prosecutor Richard Sprague had never known anything quite like Little Washington. Accustomed to the vast catacombs of Philadelphia's City Hall, where he ran an agency comparable in size to a Wall Street law firm, Sprague now found himself doing his prosecuting on the second floor of a mini-courthouse that had turn-of-the-century architecture, a gold dome with a statue of the Father of Our Country, and stained-glass windows. Sprague was only an hour away from Philadelphia by plane, but he was far from the wicked East, in a place of rolling hills, sparse population, coal mines, and country people.

In November 1971, Sprague returned to the Washington County Courthouse to prosecute the youngest of the five Yablonski murder defendants, Aubran Wayne Martin. The case offered Sprague the full panoply of the prosecutor's arena—trial by jury. It was an arena Sprague enjoyed, and its pleasure had not diminished for him after more than five thousand trials in Philadelphia.

A jury trial can be regarded as a kind of theater, with the prosecutor as the producer-director-stage manager, and the jury as the audience. Long before Martin's trial began, Sprague worked up his scenario and his cast for run-throughs. In every major trial, it was his custom to hold what he called "preps" with all state witnesses. These were preparatory meetings, not exactly rehearsals; many of the witnesses were never called onstage, and some who were found their roles to be minor. Sprague listened to witnesses and decided which testimony to use or whether to put the witnesses on the stand at all, but often his decisions were made in the courtroom. At the meetings, as always, he took no notes.

One group, made up of law-enforcement officials, would meet with Sprague in a body. The prosecutor heard each man's evidence, and watched for the unwanted volunteering of information, overlooking no shred of a significant detail: Where were the guns found? Exactly where? Where were the bullet holes? Show what the bodies looked like. After meeting together for weeks or months, the group came to regard itself as the prosecutor's "team," until finally all the players' stories merged into a cohesive whole.

Then Sprague would take another group of witnesses—laymen, persons who found a body or bodies, acquaintances who heard conversations with the accused, a citizen who accidentally made a pertinent observation. He met these witnesses individually, sifting the questions that would take these witnesses coherently through their stories on the witness stand, winnowing out inconsistencies that might tear at the fabric of a case. The meetings went on before and during trials, starting at eight-thirty at night when a case was in progress, often running until after one in the morning. And the producer-director kept his sensitivity alert to the potential impact of the witness on the jury.

The prep sessions for Martin's trial were relatively simple. Most of the thirty-two witnesses Sprague decided to use were veteran law-enforcement officials who knew their way around courtrooms, but Sprague took nothing for granted, picking over their stories as they met together at the Ramada Inn, outside Little Washington. With him to the motel he brought a small mountain of documents, evidence, and files, transported in his official car, a big, black Chrysler New Yorker his people called the Batmobile—an electronically overloaded (and municipally financed) vehicle that one of his detectives had driven from Philadelphia. One of Sprague's many rituals was to keep the car near him during major trials.

One of Sprague's main objectives at Martin's trial was to overcome, in the jurors' minds, the defendant's youthfulness, a possible source of sympathy. Martin, then twenty-three years old, still had a few pimples on his face, and wore a slicked-back 1950s hairdo that made him resemble the late actor James Dean. He had admitted committing seventy-five or eighty burglaries before turning twenty-one, but strongly denied taking part in the murder of Joseph Yablonski, and he seethed at the confession of Claude Vealey that had been made public five months before. For Sprague, one way of getting past the defendant's youthful shield was to demolish him on the witness stand; that, the prosecutor fully intended to do. But first he aimed for the selection of older jurors, and especially persons who might understand what the prosecution was trying to do. The final jury consisted of seven women and five men, and, as Sprague intended, most of them were old enough to have children the age of Yablonski's offspring.

It was not until the last juror was chosen that Sprague decided on the order of the witnesses he would call, and he decided, too, that the case would go swiftly. Many persons in the courtroom expected a two- or three-week trial, but Sprague managed to present the case for the prosecution in only a day and a half.

He led off, as he liked to when courtroom conditions were right, with his big punch. After brief testimony by Kenneth Yablonski on how he found the three bodies, Sprague tried to overwhelm the defense—and grip the jury—with an early body blow. Vealey hardly had time to state his name before Sprague was on his feet with a series of stacatto questions:

Q. Did you take part in killing Jock Yablonski?

A. Yes.

Q. Did you take part in killing Margaret Yablonski?

A. Yes.

Q. Did you take part in killing Charlotte Yablonski?

A. Yes.

Q. Do you see anyone else in the courtroom who took part in that killing with you?

A. Aubran Martin.

Q. Indicate and point him out to the jury.

A. Sitting over there at the table.

Q. You mean Martin over here?

A. Yes.

Vealey's central purpose—emphasized and reemphasized under Sprague's rapid questioning—was to finger Martin as the triggerman. Vealey said that while all three men entered the Yablonski house, it was Martin who emptied his revolver into the victims while Vealey's rifle jammed. As detail after gory detail poured from Vealey's willing lips, it became clear why Sprague had reserved the front row of the courtroom, near the jury box, for a dozen of Yablonski's relatives. Every so often the prosecutor would direct his eyes to them; and so would some of the jurors.

Aubran Martin's lawyer was a thirty-year-old Pittsburgh man named Mark Goldberg. Short, boyish-looking, with horn-rimmed glasses, he had tried only one murder case before Martin's, and in taking on the defense, he was doing a favor for a lawyer friend in Cleveland. Sprague treated Goldberg with professional distance and icy courtesy just short of disdain. (When the verdict and penalty came in, Sprague never said a word to the defense attorney.)

It appeared that Sprague achieved his intention to overwhelm the defense with Vealey's testimony. When Vealey was cross-examined by Goldberg, he repeated and reinforced the confession he had given earlier—the details of the planning, commission, and aftermath of the Yablonski murders. Vealey even admitted that he hoped to receive a reduced sentence and reward money for his confession, but he made it clear that he felt the sentence was a more tangible goal. In other words, he wasn't cooperating for money.

The presiding judge at Martin's trial seemed to be another factor on the prosecution's side—as many judges are. Charles G. Sweet had been Washington County's president judge for eight years, and he assigned himself the Yablonski case because he recognized the high drama and publicity it would afford him. He was a big man with a chunky face, like that of Charles Laughton, and the haughty bearing of a Marine colonel, which he had been. Judge Sweet was a Harvard graduate practicing in the boondocks, but he was proud to call himself a country judge. He was as fond of his witticisms as he was of the law.

Claude Vealey proved to be an effective prosecution witness. His answers were crisp and lean, stripped of any volunteered information, as though he were not out to get Martin. The impact suited Sprague, and he led Vealey through a forest of details:

Q. Had you known Martin prior to December 29, 1969?
A. Yes.
Q. For how long a period of time?
A. About six months.
Q. Now when Gilly was talking to Martin on December 29, 1969, what then happened?

A. I came into the bar and Gilly said Martin was to be the third man on the killing.

Q. I can't hear you.

A. I walked into the bar with Gilly, and Martin was there, and Gilly said Martin was to be the third man on the killing.

Q. What happened to Phillips?

A. He backed out.

Q. Is that why you're now getting a third man?

A. Yes.

Q. When Gilly said that Martin was to be the third man in the killing, what then was discussed?

A. Gilly told him who was to be killed.

Q. What did Gilly say?

A. I don't remember the exact words.

Q. As best you can recall, when you say he told Martin who was to be killed, what did he say?

A. Joseph Yablonski was the one to be killed. He lived in Clarksville, Pennsylvania, and there was fifty-two hundred dollars in money that would be split three ways.

Q. This was what Gilly said to Martin in your presence in that taproom?

A. Yes.

Q. Then what happened?

A. The next day Gilly picked me up. We went to Martin's house and picked him up.

Q. What happened? How did you know to pick up Martin?

A. Gilly told us he was planning on going to Clarksville the thirtieth.

Q. Tell the jury what did Gilly say about the next day to you and Martin?

A. He said he would pick us up the following day to go to Clarksville to kill Yablonski.

Martin sat in the courtroom, seemingly unconcerned, looking like a little boy overdressed in an ill-fitting business suit. He stared hard at Vealey, but the star witness seldom looked at the defendants' table, preferring, instead, to look at Sprague. Relaxed, one arm over the back of the witness chair, Vealey told how Martin pumped most of the bullets at the sleeping Yablonskis with the pistol, and how he, Vealey, reloaded the rifle.

Q. What were you doing with the rifle?

A. I was standing at the doorway of the other bedroom with Yablonski and his wife in it.

Q. Then what occurred?

A. Martin fired two shots.

Q. You heard the shots?

A. Yes.

Q. Where was Martin when he fired those shots?

A. Inside the bedroom.

Q. Then what happened?

A. Martin stepped over into the bedroom door of the Yablonskis and finished emptying the pistol in it.

Q. Martin emptied the pistol where?

A. At Mr. and Mrs. Yablonski.

Q. That was how many more shots by Martin at the Yablonskis?

A. Four.

Vealey then told how he heard Yablonski "making a gurgling sound." Some of the women jurors cringed as he added, "I thought he was still alive."

Q. What did you want to do?

A. Finish him.

Q. What did you do when you reloaded?

A. I walked into the bedroom, fired three more shots.

Q. At whom?

A. Joseph Yablonski.

Defense attorney Goldberg tried hard to shake Vealey's testimony, but couldn't. Vealey kept his answers as spare as they had been under Sprague's questioning and he never got rattled. Vealey came across as he was—a man who lied and stole but

was firm on one thing: he and Aubran Martin had killed Jock
Yablonski.

Goldberg conducted a lengthy and rambling cross-examination that tried the patience of both Sprague and Judge Sweet.
The judge frequently reminded Goldberg that he was going far
afield in his examination of "this guy." Goldberg also seemed
to break a cardinal rule of courtroom adversaries—never to get
on familiar terms with an opponent's witness. He frequently
addressed the witness as "Claude"—while Sprague had never
so much as approached Vealey at the witness box, treating him
as a necessary evil who happened to be cooperating with the
Commonwealth of Pennsylvania. When Goldberg questioned
Vealey about his relationship with Martin, the defense attorney
leaned on the witness stand, at the side near the jury, and almost
whispered:

Q. When did you and Buddy Martin become friends?
A. I don't remember the exact date, the exact month.
Q. How would you term your friendship with Buddy?
A. It was pretty close.
Q. Did you work together?
A. We did, yes.
Q. What kind of work?
A. Stealing.
Q. What kind?
A. Breaking and entering into houses.

If it was painful to watch such questioning of a murderer
—one looked in vain for Goldberg to show some outrage—it
was excruciating to watch the performance of Goldberg's own
star witness—his client, Buddy Martin. Why Martin ever took
the stand in his own defense is problematical. His attorney
(addressing him continually as "Buddy") built up a story of
Martin's noninvolvement that was shaky at best. Martin testified that he did not know he was leaving Cleveland to go out
on a murder job in Pennsylvania. Nor, he said, did he know
that he was to kill the Yablonskis. Rather, he was led to believe

that it was a burglary. He never entered the Yablonski house but had fallen asleep in the car—and learned only several days later that three people had been killed.

Goldberg's inexperience and Sprague's decade-long experience in murder trials were obvious when Sprague bore down on Aubran Martin. Unlike Goldberg's living-room manner in questioning Vealey, Sprague pounced on the defendant like a vulture on carrion:

Q. You remember the oath you took when you were sworn?

A. Yes, sir, I do.

Q. What was the end of it?

A. To tell the truth, the whole truth.

Q. "You shall answer to God on the last great day." Remember hearing that?

A. Yes, sir.

Q. You're pretty good at planning and scheming, aren't you?

A. I have participated in a lot of burglaries and planned burglaries and things like that. . . .

Q. According to you, Gilly and Vealey tricked you, didn't they?

A. Yes, sir, I would say I was tricked.

Q. You would say so, wouldn't you?

A. Yes, sir, that's what I said.

Q. Weren't you angry about that? They roped you into a murder, didn't they?

A. I'm pretty angry about it, yes, I am.

Q. When the FBI agents came to you and asked you about it, you didn't tell them that you had been tricked into a murder, did you?

A. I told them I——

Q. You didn't tell them you had been tricked into a murder, did you?

A. No, sir, I didn't tell them nothing.

Q. After you even heard that Vealey had opened up on you, you didn't call or send for the FBI and tell them, "Hey, wait a minute, he's the guy that tricked me into this," did you?

A. What the FBI told me, I wasn't sure whether they was telling the truth or not. I didn't want to implicate anybody. I didn't want my family killed.

Q. By your family, you mean this girl you never got a license to marry but you were living common-law with?

A. Yes, sir.

Q. Now you're not scared for her, are you?

A. Yes, sir, I am.

Q. Still are?

A. Yes, sir.

Q. Doesn't stop you from telling the story now?

Aubran Martin half-rose in the witness box, looked at the sheriff's deputies lining the courtroom doors, then sat down and flashed an angry glance at the prosecutor.

"I will never testify at one of their trials," he said. "I don't care if I stay in jail for a hundred years. I will never get up and say anything about them."

Sprague retreated a few steps to the prosecution table, let the volunteered statement echo through the courtroom, then resumed.

Q. On any other burglaries you went on, did you do target practicing before you went on the job?

A. Um, no, sir.

Q. Um, what?

A. No, sir.

Q. First time for that also?

A. Yes, sir, sure was.

Q. Were you going hunting that day?

A. No, sir.

Sprague then examined the relationship between Martin and his friend Vealey.

Q. Vealey's your friend?

A. Yes, sir, he was.

Q. Any reason for him to be lying?

A. I could think of plenty of reasons now.

Q. Tell me.

A. Well, like he said, he's up there and they offer him ten or twenty thousand dollars or something like that, from the——
This is the impression I got from his testimony.

Q. I'm not asking you the impression of the testimony. I'm saying is Vealey your friend? Do you know why he would lie against you?

A. Yes, sir, I'm trying to explain, because they offered him ten or twenty thousand dollars. He knew that what's-his-name, Phillips, had turned him in, him and Paul, for sixty thousand dollars reward total, I believe. And he knew if he couldn't come up with a good story he couldn't get out of it, plus he made it sound good enough and plus he could get some money.

Sprague turned on his heels, surveyed the jury with an expression of hopelessness and disbelief, pondered the lengthy answer, then turned again toward Martin.

Q. You think that's a good story on his part? He went in to finish Yablonski off after you shot him? You think it helps Vealey?

A. Yes, sir, I think it helps.

Q. You think it helps him to say he reloaded the gun after you; he went in and put the finishing touch on Yablonski?

A. You heard him get up and say——

Q. You think that helps him!

A. Because he won't get the electric chair.

Q. You think he what?

A. No, sir, I don't think he'll get the electric chair.

Q. You think that's the reason he's turning on you?

A. That and money and maybe something else. Maybe somebody gave his family money.

Q. Did you ever hear when one crook turns in another, society gains?

A. I don't understand that.

Martin was perspiring now in his winter suit in the warm November air, but Sprague continued to pound away. The prosecutor wound up his cross-examination by striking at the heart of the defense—the contention that Aubran Martin had been led to believe the Yablonski job was a burglary.

Q. By the way, this was the biggest job you ever went on, wasn't it?

A. At one time, I was involved in a house burglary we got twelve thousand dollars out of.

Q. Where was that?

A. In the state of Ohio.

Q. Who was with you?

A. I don't specifically remember.

Q. Oh, yes, you do. Who was with you?

A. The name, I don't. I went on so many different burglaries.

Q. This big all-time burglary of twelve thousand dollars, you surely remember who was with you on that, don't you?

A. No, sir, not specifically.

Q. You don't remember? You're under oath, Mr. Martin. Who was with you on that job?

A. I can't tell you for sure.

Q. Can't tell us for sure?

A. No, sir.

Q. Positive?

A. Positive.

Q. Really searching your memory?

A. I'm positive.

Q. Who went in the house on that job?

A. I was one of them in the house.

Q. Did you have a gun?

A. Not that I can remember. I don't believe so.

Q. You're not sure?

A. I'm not sure. I said I can't remember so I'm not sure.

Q. Is this the biggest job, the Yablonski job, you were ever on where you were guaranteed money in advance?

A. It was the first time I was ever guaranteed money whether anything was gotten or not, yes.

Q. That's all.

The long cross-examination ended late at night, but as Sprague thought it over, he became concerned about his own performance against the youthful defendant. Sprague was apprehensive that the jury, on reflection, would get to thinking about Martin's statements as to Vealey's motives—the fact that Vealey might be lying to save his own neck. Sprague grew concerned that the young man he called a baby-faced killer might become, in the jury's eyes, a put-upon kid whose mouth would melt butter.

The next day, two convicts from a Pennsylvania prison went on the stand to tell how Martin had admitted to them his role in the shootings. Back Aubran Martin went to the witness stand to deny their testimony, giving Sprague another chance to hit hard at Martin's view of the state's star witness.

"I'm saying," Martin testified, his voice rising, "that Vealey is liable to get up here and say anything. He knows if he don't make a good story, he's going to get the electric chair."

Sprague drew near the defendant and lowered his normally loud voice.

"What about you?" Sprague asked. "If you don't make a good story, what do you think is going to happen to you?"

"I don't know."

"You don't know?"

"No, sir."

"That's all."

And for Sprague, that was all. He was now convinced that Martin's own testimony convicted him. In claiming that he had fallen asleep in the car while the others killed Yablonski, Martin had entered a legal mousetrap. Under Pennsylvania's felony-murder doctrine, anyone who takes part in a felony leading to murder is as guilty as the one who does the killing. Judge Sweet agreed that the point was crucial, and when he gave his legal instructions to the jury, the judge spent considerable time discussing the felony-murder doctrine. When Goldberg interrupted the judge's charges to the jury on this point,

Sweet chastised him and went on to elaborate on the rule.

Indeed, it seemed as if Judge Sweet seldom bent over backward to help the defense in Martin's trial. Tending to be self-centered and impressed with his own one-liners, Sweet frequently told the jury that the legal maneuvers were "part of the game." He also told them that when he and the lawyers held sidebar conferences out of the jury's hearing, they were "not just chewing the fat." The peak of Judge Sweet's courtroom wit came when the two sides were getting ready to give their closing speeches to the jury. Noting that it was late in the morning, the judge reminded the lawyers of the approaching lunch hour. Then he turned his Charles Laughton face to the jurors and declaimed:

"All right, the next stage of the game is oral argument. At this procedural stage, you receive addresses from each side, and those are important for you because they're the stage of the game where the attorney pulls together his facts and theories and explains to you why various pieces of evidence are significant and gives you his reasons as to whom you should believe and whom you should not believe.

"Now, let's see if we can figure out a way of doing this that will divide our time fairly. Well, how long do you need, Mr. Goldberg?"

"Approximately twenty minutes to a half-hour, Your Honor."

"It is now eleven o'clock," said the judge. "Can each of you take approximately a half an hour so we can hear both arguments before lunch and feed the jury reasonably close to twelve o'clock?"

"Your Honor," said Sprague, "I talk as I talk. It's very difficult for me to put a time on it. I would hope to be able to be completed before lunch if defense counsel is finished in about twenty minutes or so. That's all I can say."

"Let me urge on both of you," said Judge Sweet, "without fixing a mechanical time limit, very few souls are saved after twenty minutes. You probably remember what Hubert

Humphrey said, 'The mind can no longer receive, when the seat can no longer endure.' "

Aubran Martin looked a bit uncomfortable as the judge flashed a broad smile to the jury. And the jury did get to lunch on time; after hearing Sprague tear apart the defendant.

"They wanted someone who would be a tough punk who wouldn't give two hoots for human life," Sprague told the jurors, "and that's why they picked this defendant here. Buddy boy! The con artist! Just an adorable little boy!" Sprague snarled. Was the jury reluctant to find him guilty and then impose the death penalty because politicians wouldn't carry it out? Sprague warned that they, too, could be victims of "assassins in the night."

The jury required only an hour and a half to find Aubran Martin guilty of three counts of murder in the first degree. The death penalty was still legal in Pennsylvania, and the next day the jurors met again to decide that phase of the case—the separate deliberation that had been established in one of Sprague's cases in Philadelphia. Defense attorney Goldberg pleaded for mercy, but Sprague demanded the death penalty. He urged that a reluctant state government must carry out capital punishment. In another forty minutes of deliberation, the jurors rejected life in prison for Martin and decided he must die in the electric chair.

Martin had discarded the ill-fitting dark suit and tie he wore during the trial, and now, coming back to hear the penalty, he shocked many spectators by wearing a gold open-necked sweater-blouse, garish striped bell-bottoms, and a saucy navy blue neckerchief. He no longer looked baby-faced.

It was high noon on a Saturday in Little Washington. Although it was mid-November, a sky of a summer blue arched gently over the gold-domed Washington County Courthouse. As sheriff's deputies took Martin out a back door, Richard Sprague came down the courthouse steps to Main Street, moving deliberately, not hurriedly, and showing no sign of gloating over his sixty-sixth murder conviction. His black Chrysler with the four antennas waited at curbside; the Batmobile was ready to be taken back to Philadelphia with its storehouse of evidence, documents, and photographs.

Television cameras and reporters were poised on the sidewalk to get Sprague's reactions now that Martin's trial was over. He told them the verdict should be a warning to others: "We intend to get *all* those behind this crime."

Then Sprague went back to the Ramada Inn, had a glass of tomato juice, and began thinking about Paul Gilly's trial, coming up in three months.

On a Friday a week later, Paul Gilly sat in the Western Penitentiary at Pittsburgh, mulling over a visit from some "agents" Sprague had sent after the Martin trial verdict. They told Gilly they wanted information about others "up the line" in the Yablonski murders, and they left asking Gilly to "think about it." Sprague did not expect an answer from Gilly at that point, nor did he need one.

In Washington, D.C., that same Friday in November 1971, there was good news for coal miners. President Nixon's Pay Board had just approved the first-year phase of a new three-year contract for the soft-coal industry. The contract called for a 16.8 percent boost in wages in the first year, a whopping 37.8 percent over three years—far in excess of the Pay Board's guideline of 5.5 percent. Once again, the international president of the United Mine Workers of America had delivered to his rank and file, but in the pictures that moved over the wire services that night, Tony Boyle was not smiling.

5

"I Have Something to Say"

A DEFENDANT in a criminal case finds himself
at the mercy of three people—the judge, the prosecutor, and
his own lawyer. He can scarcely do anything about the first two.
The judge is likely to be a former prosecutor himself, and, if
not, he is likely to be on good terms with the prosecutor, whom
he sees frequently. The defendant's lawyer tries to ingratiate
himself as much as he can with the man in the black robes—he
may even invite judges to parties at his home—but try as he
will, the defense attorney often concludes that the cards of
justice are stacked against his man.

The deck was not stacked against Paul Eugene Gilly, the
third accused triggerman in the Yablonski murder case, but the
onrushing events of the case tended to overwhelm him. In
Cleveland, Gilly had retained, for himself and his wife Annette,
a lawyer named Gerald Gold, a leading criminal attorney.

When Gilly came to trial in late February 1972, he had not
seen his wife for two years. (Sprague had insisted on separate
trials to increase pressure on both of them.) After being taken
into custody in Cleveland, they were kept in separate jails in
Ohio, and then isolated from each other when they were
brought to Pennsylvania. Unknown to Gilly, Annette was seeking a way to get out of jail, and unknown to him, she found
one.

Before Gilly's trial they had a grotesque kind of reunion.

They were brought in handcuffs to the Washington County Court for a joint appearance on a legal matter crucial to both. The problem was their retaining the same lawyer and how that might affect any future appeals on their behalf. To resolve the point, they had to agree to waive any rights to appeal on the question.

As they stood side by side in the big dark courtroom before Judge Sweet—Annette Gilly in heels, almost as tall as her six-foot husband—their hands met at the bar, out of sight of the judge and most spectators. Yes, each said in hardly audible tones, they would agree "from now until the end of time" to waive their right of appeal on the basis of having the same attorney. "From now until the end of time," the judge repeated. For a moment the brief proceeding was like a nightmarish parody of a wedding ceremony. As they were led out by sheriff's deputies, back to their separate prisons to await trial, their glances met briefly in an expression of mutual anguish, but the only words they spoke were to the court.

Their attorney, Gold, pressed ahead with his pretrial motions for Paul Gilly. A balding, affable man who had developed a reputation for taking and winning unpopular cases in the civil liberties field, Gold attempted to milk the beneficence of the law for his client. But he was up against fearful odds.

For one thing, the Aubran Martin trial, three months earlier, had produced massive publicity on the Yablonski case in southwestern Pennsylvania. From Pittsburgh to the West Virginia border, there wasn't a newspaper or radio or television station that had not given the case detailed prominence. Gold and his co-counsel in Washington County, Samuel Rodgers, contended that their man could not get a fair trial in Washington County. At one stage, they asked Judge Sweet to subpoena records, clippings, and films of Pittsburgh news media, and they requested that the county pay the cost for a small truck to pick up the items. Judge Sweet agreed that it would require a truck to collect the material, but he turned down the request. He concluded that the pretrial publicity, while massive, had been restrained.

The defense lawyers then challenged the method of selecting juries in Washington County. Jurors' names were turned in by committeemen representing the Democratic and Republican parties. The defense argued that this method was political, and that it restricted the sample of jurors; few young people or blacks stood a chance of going on a jury panel. Judge Sweet rejected this request, too, in his accustomed trenchant style: "What is a political worker? Is anybody who says to his brother-in-law, 'Why don't you vote for Muskie?' a political worker? . . . These jurors were not chosen from the rolls of registered electors, but only from the whole body of qualified electors. They are Republicans and Democrats in substantially the same proportion that these two breeds of cat are found in the community at large."

But there were some who felt that Judge Sweet's own "breed of cat" weighted the even-handed balance of justice. Like Prosecutor Sprague, he was a conservative Democrat. Like Prosecutor Sprague, he felt that the prisons of Pennsylvania were too lenient toward felons; indeed, Sweet was then actively lobbying against prerelease and furlough programs for inmates. Like Prosecutor Sprague, Judge Sweet was a staunch "law-and-order man." And like Sprague he knew the Yablonskis.

Sweet's ruling upholding Washington County's jury-selection system paved the way for Paul Gilly's trial to begin. It turned out to be Judge Sweet's last jury trial in the Yablonski murder case.

Richard Sprague had a number of things on his mind besides Paul Gilly when he boarded a jet plane in Philadelphia to begin a return engagement in the Yablonski murder case. In Philadelphia, a new mayor had just been sworn in—the tough cop Frank Rizzo, with whom Sprague enjoyed a close relationship. Rizzo was elected while Sprague was out of town prosecuting

Aubran Martin, and one of Rizzo's first statements on taking office was that the Yablonski case showed the need for enforcing the death penalty in Pennsylvania. Sprague, though equally firm on the use of capital punishment as a deterrent to crime, had to smile on hearing Rizzo declare that perhaps Philadelphia should have its own electric chair—and that he, the mayor, would be delighted to pull the switch.

Sprague also reflected on the mounting legal troubles of Tony Boyle. In the District of Columbia, the Justice Department was moving to prosecute Boyle on federal charges of illegally giving United Mine Workers money to the 1968 campaigns of Hubert Humphrey and other candidates, a violation of the Corrupt Practices Act. The amount involved totaled $49,000 in union money, but Boyle contended that it had been standard union practice for years. In some quarters, there was a suspicion that the Nixon administration, that spring of 1972, was sending out a message to unions through the charges against Boyle: Stay away from the 1972 presidential election campaign. The publicity surrounding Boyle's case, though, inevitably linked Boyle's name to the Yablonski murder case in southwestern Pennsylvania, and that didn't seem to bother the prosecutor in the least.

The Yablonski case was beginning to jell with outside events. Besides the prosecution of Boyle on the political-contribution charges, Yablonski's followers were gaining strength in their attempts to overturn Boyle as president of the United Mine Workers. Their support within the union was increasing as thousands of coal miners recognized the true nature of their union leadership. Their legal challenges to that leadership were being heard. And in court, their argument for a new election seemed to be making progress.

In this atmosphere, Sprague assembled his "team" once more in Little Washington. He proceeded on the assumption that Paul Gilly, unlike Aubran Martin, would not get on the witness stand. Therefore, Claude Vealey would again be a star witness, but Sprague planned to buttress his testimony with another "big punch"—the story of James Charles Phillips, the fourth man in the lower levels of the case. As Gilly went on trial, Sprague concluded that the prosecution was on the brink of cracking the mystery of why Jock Yablonski was killed and who ordered his assassination.

By the time of Gilly's trial, Claude Vealey was a practiced witness. For the third time, he ambled into Courtroom Number One and easily rattled off his story of his role in the Yablonski murders. He never showed any strain or nervousness as he sat in the witness box testifying against Gilly before a jam-packed crowd of several hundred spectators. Matter-of-factly, the casually dressed Vealey, his bulging biceps revealed by a polo shirt, pointed his finger at Gilly and told how the two of them and Aubran Martin pumped bullets into the sleeping Yablonskis.

For Sprague, Vealey's testimony was not enough. For the first time in the case, the prosecutor called on James Charles Phillips, who even then was under indictment in Cleveland on a charge of raping a four-year-old girl—the daughter of his girl friend. (Phillips was convicted and is now serving a life term in Ohio for that crime.) Knowing that Gilly wouldn't testify and thus be eligible for demolishment on the witness stand, Sprague asked Phillips to unload his tale of how he was recruited by Gilly to stalk Jock Yablonski.

Phillips was taller and heavier than Claude Vealey, and had a habit of cracking his knuckles when he tried to remember details of the case. He had short brown hair, thick muscles, and only the dimmest knowledge of how to read and write. He seldom smiled. Like the accused triggermen, Phillips had a southern accent (he was from West Virginia, and had migrated to Cleveland's Appalachian ghetto). The tale he told of what happened between July and December 1969 contained elements of black comedy—fantastic bumblings, false starts, mistaken identities—and enough horror to rivet the eyes of the jury, the courtroom spectators, and the Yablonski family on his impassive face.

"Claude Vealey approached me one day at the Family Tavern," Phillips said under Sprague's questioning. "He asked me if I wanted to make some easy money. I asked him how first, and he said he couldn't tell me. He had to talk to somebody else.

"It was the following day, I think, Vealey came upstairs and got me. We went down to the tavern. Paul Gilly bought us all a beer and we went over to a table. He told me that he had a contract. He said he had a contract on a man who was in Pennsylvania, and he was a high United Mine official. And he asked me if I was interested. And I told him I had to think about it—forty-two hundred dollars split three ways, plus he said there was money in the house and a coin collection or something.

"He set up a trip to Washington, D.C. because Yablonski worked there."

Fortunately, the trip ended before it started. Vealey and Phillips got arrested for a burglary in Youngstown. They were in jail about a week. The contract wasn't beginning auspiciously. Gilly got Vealey out on bail and somebody else sprang Phillips. Off they went from Cleveland to Washington, Gilly at the wheel in his 1965 maroon Chevy.

"Gilly had a briefcase," Phillips related, "and it had a thirty-eight snub-nose in it and couple of other guns. And he had a newspaper clipping in it of Yablonski with a few other people in it. It had an arrow drawn in it. He showed it to me and Vealey and said that this is the guy that we're supposed to get. It's the one he had the contract on.

"We proceeded to Washington. We got in there about six or seven o'clock that morning and we looked up—well, Gilly knows the way to the United Mine Workers building. He's got the address and everything. We parked in front, went in the restaurant and had breakfast right beside of the building.

"We ate breakfast and Joseph Yablonski was supposed to come in there or eat or have coffee. He didn't show up. So Vealey, Gilly, and myself left and drove around for about an hour, and Gilly made a call . . . to Yablonski's office.

"The secretary told Gilly that he was up on the Hill, and none of us knew what that meant. And so Gilly looks up the address of his [Yablonski's] son's house. He come up with two addresses. We found the one by a hospital, I forget the name of it, but he made a call—Gilly made a call and there wasn't anybody home. We went by the house and couldn't see nobody.

"There was another address off of Old Mill road. He looked for it for maybe two or three hours and couldn't find that address, so we give it up for that night.

"We went back downtown and we developed brake trouble with the car, and we went to an all-night parts place and bought some [brake] shoes. We went to a station and I put the shoes on there. And Gilly made a call from there—his wife Lucy [Annette].

"We drove around for a couple hours after that. I went to sleep in the back seat and last I remembered that night was pulling in the station and Gilly giving the guy some money to wake us up the next morning."

The guns were in a briefcase in the front seat, Phillips related, and the next morning they drove out to Bethesda, Maryland, to the house of Joseph Yablonski, Jr. Gilly stayed in the car, down the street from the house, and Vealey and Phillips went up to the house.

"And what were you supposed to do?" Sprague asked Phillips.

"We were supposed to find out if Yablonski was there."

"And if he was there, what were you to do?"

"Supposed to kill him."

"Who told you that?"

"Gilly."

Armed with two guns, Vealey and Phillips knocked on the door and a woman answered.

"Vealey done all the talking," said Phillips. "The woman answered the door and he asked for Joseph Yablonski. And she asked us in and she went and got her husband."

It turned out to be the wrong Yablonski—it was Jock's son

Chip and the woman was his wife Shirley. Chip, suspicious of the strangers, told them that his father was in Scranton, Pennsylvania.

"We left, me and Vealey did," said Phillips, "and went back down to the car with Gilly. And so Gilly wanted to go on to Scranton, so we left for Scranton and got into Scranton sometime in the evening.

"We stopped at a restaurant and had supper and Paul Gilly got the phone book and looked up Yablonski's telephone number and address. He asked the waitress if she knew him and she said no. And he went and looked for the house. We found it but I think it took us about three hours. It was the wrong house and everything; we started to leave.

"We stopped at a bar and had a couple hamburgers and a couple beers, shot some pool, and I think there was something on TV about Yablonski, and Gilly called the paper. And they told him that Yablonski left town already.

"So we're leaving. We stop at the station to fill up with gas and Paul says that he is going to call Lucy [Annette] and make sure of the address, that he had it wrote down. He said he had the address, the right address, wrote down at home.

"Gilly called, and said that she couldn't find it, that she couldn't find it and she'd have to get in touch with Tony. Lucy would have to get in touch with Tony, and he would have to call her back in twenty minutes.

"Gilly called his wife back, and she told him that it was Clarksville, Pennsylvania. And she told him at the time that we just missed Tony in Washington, D.C.

"We went to Clarksville. It was about six in the morning, six-thirty, so we stopped at the telephone booth. Gilly looked up Yablonski's phone number."

"By the way," Sprague asked, "how many days have elapsed in this business up to now?"

"About three," said Phillips. They had driven from Cleveland to Washington, D.C., and from Bethesda to Scranton, in northeastern Pennsylvania, across Pennsylvania to Clarksville near the West Virginia border, and they had yet to lay eyes on their quarry.

"Gilly gets out," said Phillips, "looks up the address and the phone number and takes the book and just brings the book back to the car. We looked for the house. We couldn't find it, so we drove down the road for two or three mile [*sic*], pulled over and went to sleep and we slept for almost three hours. So we got back down to town by the fire station, and Gilly calls the house, the Yablonski house.

"And his wife answers and says that he isn't there, that he is still in Scranton. Gilly wanted to go back to Scranton. Me and Vealey, we refused. We went home."

So the first trip in pursuit of Yablonski was a bummer. By Phillips's account, it had covered hundreds of miles, and the three contract men were worn out and hadn't found their man, and they had left all kinds of footprints behind them. Undaunted, they set out from Cleveland again.

"We went back to Pennsylvania about the last of October," Phillips said. "To kill Yablonski. It was on the weekend. We got down there, I think it was a Saturday. Gilly called the house and his wife said he wasn't home. We drove around figuring that he'll be in sometime that day.

"We drive around, killing time, waiting, maybe he will come in, you know. It's up in the evening, and we go down to a bar. We stop to get something to eat and Gilly says he's going to make a call to Lucy, his wife, and find out for sure where Yablonski is at.

"He came back inside and said he would have to call back in about fifteen or twenty minutes because she had to call Tony to find out.

"He came back and told us that Yablonski was still in Washington, D.C. We went back home."

Now they took another trip—to Tennessee, where the three of them broke into a house and stole some shotguns, rifles, and pistols. One of them was a nickel-plated pistol, which Sprague now showed Phillips in the courtroom—the gun that had helped kill Yablonski. Phillips nodded and said that was it.

In November 1969 they made a third trip, this time with a .38 snub-nose and two .25 automatics.

"It was sometime in the evening on a weekend, and Gilly called the Yablonski house, and there was no answer, so he had already told us if there wasn't anybody home we would ride by and rob the house anyway.

"There wasn't anybody home, so he took me and Vealey by and dropped us off. He dropped us off down the road from the house; me and Vealey walked up to the door, and we was knocking on the front door and the paperboy come down the road. He left the paper and left. We went around to the back door or the side. I knocked on the kitchen door and Vealey checked the other door going to the back of the living room, and in between the doors, there was a dog. It didn't bark or anything, and the other door was unlocked, so we went in the house."

Vealey and Phillips searched the Yablonski house, but Phillips said that it was another fruitless trip. There was no money or coin collection, as he had been led to believe, and what was worse, when he and Vealey got outside, Paul Gilly and the car were gone. It was four or five o'clock and growing dark on the country road, and the two started hitchhiking. Pretty soon Gilly picked them up, and they were off to Cleveland again.

But Phillips had had it with Paul Gilly—three trips and hundreds of miles of driving all over Pennsylvania and nothing to show for it, and Phillips's role ended with a fit of pique.

"I told him I was dropping out," said Phillips. "I didn't want to do it because he had run off and left me."

Sprague immediately called to the witness stand a sixteen-year-old girl named Kathy Rygle. Kathy had long brown hair, spoke in a low voice, turned a clean bright face to the jury—in short, she was the picture of honesty. Her brief testimony provided a dramatic contrast with that of the burly Phillips concerning his pursuit of the elusive Yablonski.

Kathy lived in Clarksville, a country block from the Yablonski farmhouse. She remembered a day in 1969, around Thanksgiving, the month Phillips said he made his last trip to the Yablonski house. She was playing with her cousin that day, and the two girls invented a new game for themselves. They began taking down license numbers of passing cars. They wrote down the state, make of car, and color of dozens of vehicles. In court, Sprague showed Kathy a piece of paper, the very paper she had been writing on that day. There it was, the fifth car on the list: "CX457, Ohio, Caprice, maroon," the car registered under the name of Paul Gilly's wife. Even the normally unflappable Judge Sweet was flabbergasted. "Don't you think that we're all entitled to some explanation of how such a thing turns up after two years and some months?" he asked Sprague.

"Good police work, Your Honor," replied the prosecutor, a broad grin lighting up his face.

Instead of putting Paul Gilly on the witness stand, his lawyers presented a parade of his relatives—not including his incarcerated wife—who testified to his good name and character. Unfortunately for Gilly, many of them lived in Indiana, making them unaware of the company he kept in Cleveland. They knew he was a hard-working house painter, but they didn't know he was a fence whose friends included the likes of Claude Vealey, Aubran Martin, and James Charles Phillips.

Judge Sweet made a warning to the opposing lawyers—the line he liked so much in the Martin trial, "Very few souls are saved after twenty minutes"—and defense attorney Gerald Gold got up and lashed out at the "web of circumstances" that had been woven by the prosecution witnesses. Gold said that Phillips had been offered promises and a reward and he was "laying it on harder."

But the special prosecutor mustered his most vivid rhetoric
to demand that the jury find Paul Gilly guilty of murder in the
first degree. "The man who recruited a pack of rattlesnakes,"
exclaimed Sprague, pointing at the defendant. Then, turning to
Gold and his associate, Samuel Rodgers: "These lawyers could
talk the stripes off a zebra. We are not going to let hoodlums
and assassins walk into courts filled with bleeding hearts, and
walk out free. Nobody's painting a halo on the likes of a Phillips
or a Vealey or a Martin. They were lured by this defendant here.
He's the older person."

With a final shot at Paul Gilly as "the captain of the enterprise," Sprague urged the jurors to "stand up straight and true"
for the community. At 2:40 P.M. on March 1, 1972, Gilly's jury
left Courtroom Number One to begin its deliberations.

Six hours later, there was a stir in the semidarkened courthouse. Word was out that the jury was coming back. Quickly
an audience gathered in the courtroom. Outside, along Main
Street in Little Washington, a soft rain fell, and through the
open courthouse windows, one could hear the whine of a police
siren. The courtroom was humid, and many of the spectators
fanned themselves with newspapers or handkerchiefs.

From the left-hand door at the front of the courtroom,
Sprague entered first, looking calm because he had never left
the courthouse and had been napping in a back room of the
district attorney's office after finishing his dinner—the usual
chocolate malted. From the right-hand side came defense attorney Gold; affable as ever, he nodded to the area of the front
row, at no one in particular. A moment later came his associate,
Rodgers.

The sheriff and his deputies brought Paul Gilly in. He did
not acknowledge his nine relatives sitting on the third row and
did not look up as Judge Sweet climbed to the bench. Gilly sat
erect and dignified at the defense table, his chin resting on his
left hand.

The twelve jurors filed in, none of them looking at the

defendant, and lined up at the bar before Judge Sweet, who asked them if they had reached a verdict. "We have," some of them mumbled, and by way of a court crier it was read: guilty of all three counts of murder in the first degree.

Gilly's left hand twitched slightly, but he did not move as the jury was led back to its box on the left. Women members of Gilly's family began to weep; members of the Yablonski family sat motionless, all eyes on the jury. The lawyers requested a sidebar conference with the judge.

Ten minutes later, they began the penalty phase of the proceeding—the separate jury decision on life in prison or death in the electric chair, a procedure that would soon be on its way out, by order of the Supreme Court of the United States. Defense co-counsel Rodgers spoke sincerely and passionately for mercy. "Enough blood has been spilled in this case," he said. "You will do no good by putting Paul Gilly to death. I beg of you—spare his life."

Sprague rose, drew near the jury box, and his first words were in praise of Rodgers. "One of the finest speeches I ever heard," said the prosecutor, and he meant it; but he was there to demand the death penalty.

Sprague again made reference to politicians who would not let the switch be pulled on the electric chair: "God help us all if they flinch from imposing the law." He urged the jurors to "stand tall and true" and render a verdict of the death penalty.

At 9:40 P.M., with the soft rain still falling and flapping window shades providing the only sounds in the dark night, the jurors were led out of the courtroom to make another decision. They could not agree that night. At eleven o'clock, Judge Sweet, no longer wearing his robes, called the parties together in the courtroom and announced that he was sending the jury back to its hotel until the next morning. Everyone in the courtroom was exhausted.

Sprague was disappointed. He might have waited until the next morning to begin the arguments on Gilly's penalty, but he had pressed on in order to capitalize on his momentum. He had felt that the darkness of the night, the rain outside, and even the exhaustion of the jury, which had begun its work fourteen hours earlier, had worked in his favor. He wanted to continue the mood of the courtroom, but for once his supersitition about not leaving the courthouse during a jury deliberation had to be breached.

The next morning the rain continued. The jury was back in the courthouse at nine-thirty. Paul Gilly's family was gone, most of them back to Indianapolis. The Yablonski family members took up their posts in the front row of the courtroom.

A few minutes after eleven, the jury returned to the courtroom. Paul Gilly was brought in from the jail, again wearing the dark funeral suit and tie he had worn throughout his trial. Again the jurors avoided looking at him.

When they were asked what their verdict was, some of them didn't wait for the court crier to read the slip of paper. It came out in one word: "Death!"

Gasps went up in the courtroom. A wire-service reporter stood up and, for no apparent reason, raised a clenched fist. Then someone else stood up; it was Paul Gilly.

"I wish to speak, please," he said, but his two lawyers quickly pulled him down. He rose again: "I have something to say." But this time, two deputy sheriffs grabbed Gilly by the shoulders and plunked him into his chair, still protesting. The courtroom was on the brink of turmoil as spectators asked each other what Gilly was saying. No one was sure. The court stenographer looked puzzled, while the speechless defense attorneys looked at each other. Sprague got up to address the court. He asked that the verdict be recorded, a routine procedure, but he was taking no chances on a legal oversight. One of the defense attorneys asked that the jurors be polled, also a routine procedure, and each affirmed the death penalty.

Judge Sweet then made a speech to the jurors, congratulating them for upholding the traditions of Anglo-Saxon justice.

He praised the opposing lawyers, and now Gilly and the jurors were led out their separate ways and the trial was over.

A number of persons rushed forward to Judge Sweet and the court stenographer, wanting to know what Gilly had said. The judge, with a forbidding expression, said, "His words were inaudible, and they will be recorded as such in the record." The stenographer nodded.

Sprague hurried out of the courtroom to notify some FBI agents of what had happened. He felt that Gilly might be in a talking mood, and he wanted the agents to be at Gilly's cell immediately, in case the time was ripe.

Joseph Yablonski's son Chip walked into the district attorney's office just as the FBI men were being dispatched. Slowly, he put out his hand to Sprague, and after a few seconds said one word: "Thanks."

There were different accounts of what Gilly had tried to say. At first, Sprague thought he had heard Gilly declare he would not take all this by himself. That may have been wishful thinking on the part of the prosecutor, for the sheriff who had been with the defendant for weeks and who had stood closest to him at the abortive outburst in the courtroom reported that Paul Gilly's words were:

"If they can live with their conscience, so can I."

6

Annette and Silous

THE CONVICTION OF Paul Gilly and the death penalty the jury imposed had a traumatic effect on his wife, Annette. That was one of the effects Sprague intended, and to reinforce the message he told reporters after Gilly's trial that the Yablonski murder case was far from over. "If Gilly had not received the death penalty," Sprague said in his posttrial statement, "*they* would have thought they beat the case." And he emphasized the word "they."

And what about the man named Tony? the reporters asked Sprague. Vealey had been the first to mention Tony, and now Phillips had mentioned him, too; but who was he? How close was the prosecution to identifying the mysterious Tony and finding him?

"I've said repeatedly this case goes far beyond the five defendants who have been apprehended," Sprague replied. "We're gonna get all the people who initiated this plan of assassination. I expect that eventually we will get to this man named Tony. And I'm sure that Tony tonight will be much more fearful and much more expectant that we will get to him than he was last night. I think Tony may be a little more worried tonight than he was yesterday."

In the Washington County jail, Annette Gilly tried to maintain her composure, but the nervous way she averted her eyes from cops and strangers showed that she was having a difficult time. She had good reason to be afraid, even aside from her husband's conviction. It was March of 1972 and she had been under arrest for twenty-five months. She had been taken into custody in Cleveland, held in prison without bail, shifted from jail to jail in Ohio, extradited to Pennsylvania, and was now a semipermanent resident of a dreary turn-of-the-century lockup in Little Washington, where the temporary male prisoners and even some of the jailers stared at her, the only female in the place.

Her husband's trial stirred fears that she had pushed aside since her confinement in Ohio. Hers would be the next trial, and her father's would follow. She loathed the thought of indefinite confinement—she was only thirty-two and had a teen-age son—and just as important, she wanted at all costs not to harm her ailing father. She scarcely thought about her newly convicted husband Paul. Now it was Annette Gilly and Silous Huddleston against Richard Sprague.

Sprague considered Annette Gilly the toughest woman he'd faced in fifteen years as a prosecutor. She was about five feet seven, almost as tall as Sprague himself, and weighed around one hundred forty pounds. She had long thin legs, flowing blonde hair, blue eyes, and a thin, mean mouth. She had a Tennessee accent and a deceptively shy and polite manner; she always referred to the prosecutor as "Mr. Sprague" and to Jock Yablonski as "Mr. Yablonski." Her charms notwithstanding, Sprague preferred to concentrate on Annette Gilly's fears.

She was afraid of a long jail term. She was afraid of the possibility of receiving the electric chair (the Supreme Court hadn't yet ruled on its constitutionality). She was afraid of what the United Mine Workers establishment might do to her. And she was afraid of involving her father, Silous Huddleston.

Annette was Silous's baby. He called her Lucy. He turned to her in times of need, and she responded with the love and affection that she considered wasted on her cold husband Paul. Annette had a warm relationship with her father. When the murder of Joseph Yablonski was being set up in the summer and fall of 1969, Annette, in Cleveland, took phone calls from Huddleston, in Tennessee, and she turned to him for instructions when she was arrested. His instructions: "Whatever you do, Lucy, don't talk."

Silous Huddleston represented more than a father to her. He represented power—the power that District 19 of the UMW held over thousands of coal miners. In the small towns of the Appalachian coal fields of District 19, the union was a powerful presence, a source of jobs and hospital admission cards, pensions and political clout. The union poured money into organizing campaigns against recalcitrant nonunion coal companies, and it spent heavily in local political campaigns. Though Huddleston had never gone past the eighth grade, Annette knew he represented an awesome power. As the president of a union local made up of pensioned miners, he wielded considerable strength in everyday matters. One word from Silous and half a hundred elderly miners trembled. He was their contact with the international headquarters of the union, a far-off power in Washington, which most miners never get to see. That power, embodied in Silous Huddleston in eastern Tennessee, was more fearful than that of the White House.

Prosecutor Sprague recognized that Silous Huddleston was his link to higher-ups in the union. How to break that link? How to crack that coughing, crafty old man whose body was wracked by five or six diseases ranging from heart ailments to coal miner's black lung? Sprague, son of a psychoanalyst father and a psychiatrist mother, saw that Annette's fears were the touchstone. Her fears of jail, of the electric chair, of her father, and of the union had to be worked on. His plan was to cut through those fears and see where they could be turned to the prosecution's advantage.

In her prison cell after her husband's trial, Annette Gilly talked only to her lawyer, Gerald Gold, who had unsuccessfully defended Paul. There were rumors that she had indirect contact with her father and that Huddleston passed the word to her: "Stand firm, Lucy, you'll be killed if you open your mouth." But the conviction of Paul Gilly, the imposition of the death penalty, the determination of Sprague and his agents, and finally the chance of making a deal—these factors caused Annette to cave in. Three weeks after Paul's trial, Gerald Gold met with Sprague. Annette Gilly would tell what she knew about the murder of Joseph Yablonski.

Sprague reasoned that Annette Gilly was likely to lie, or at least to withhold vital details. He wanted her confession, but he wanted it unadulterated. He came up with an extraordinary method of getting the full story. One morning in March 1972, as spring warmth was descending on Little Washington, Sprague ordered Annette spirited out of southwestern Pennsylvania. A caravan of state police cars swept across the state, three hundred miles to the east, to Philadelphia, with the tall blonde under guard. There Sprague could spend a couple of weeks having her interviewed, and subjecting her statements to lie-detector tests. Sprague was taking no chances: the testimony of Annette Gilly could end the Yablonski murder case, or shift it to a new plane.

"At the beginning," Sprague explained, "she just wanted to give the meagerest details. If there were, say, five meetings about murdering Yablonski, she would tell you about one. But we were talking about an assassination that was planned over a period of six months or more, with all kinds of arrangements made and different people involved. It was important to get the full story from her, and I knew it would be a long-drawn-out procedure. It occurred to me to take daily lie-detector tests as she unfolded the story, and I could only do that and review the story near my office in Philadelphia. So we took her where I could have more control over the situation."

In Philadelphia, Annette Gilly was put up at the Sheraton Hotel, guarded by more than twenty Pennsylvania state police-men and -women and by FBI agents. It was a secret operation, agreed to by her lawyer and Judge Sweet.

At the hotel, she talked, drank lots of black coffee, and talked some more. She said the murder plot was set up in the summer of 1969 by a phone call from her father in Tennessee to her husband in Cleveland. Her father wanted Paul Gilly to recruit the killers. Paul wanted to see the money, so she and Paul drove down to Tennessee, and Huddleston counted out five thousand dollars.

Every word of her story was checked out on the polygraph. At his Philadelphia headquarters three blocks from the hotel, Sprague read the daily reports and saw significant omissions. He wasn't satisfied, and every so often he dropped into the hotel, with words like this: "You came here with a promise to tell all you know. There's been an indication by the lie-detector tests that you're holding back. If that's the way you want it to be, we're going to send you right back, and we'll proceed with your trial. It's tell all or nothing. You're gonna tell all, or you're gonna go to jail for the rest of your life."

Annette Gilly sat in a wooden chair in the hotel room. In the back of her mind was the thought that the prosecutor would take her to trial and demand the death penalty. Her knee-length skirt moved up a bit as she squirmed in the chair before the deep-voiced Sprague, and she tried to persuade him that she was telling all she knew. Then she put her hands over her face and began to cry. Stoically, Sprague waited it out, then resumed: "That's a lot of nonsense. We know what you know. You're gonna tell us, or you're gonna go to jail for the rest of your life. And you're gonna get no consideration, no recommendation from the court."

Annette Gilly stopped crying. She leaned forward in her chair, then straightened up, became almost coquettish, playing out what one observer called her "second routine." It didn't work. She saw that Sprague was not going to accept half-truths or withheld details. She began to talk some more, and the polygraph checked every word.

Sprague's man at the polygraph was Joseph Brophy, a Philadelphia police lie-detector expert for nearly twenty years. Brophy spent eight days checking Annette's story on the machine, and said afterward that he had never run into a tougher witness.

"It never took us so long to get information from a cooperative witness," Brophy said. "We would spend two, three, four hours at a stretch, going over her answers on the machine, and at the end of each session she was sweating like a man. She must have had iron kidneys, because she never had to go to the ladies' room."

There were many things to verify in Annette's story before it could be presented in court: her husband's role in the murders, her father's participation, the source of the payoff money, any possible involvement of the United Mine Workers, places, dates. She was grilled for hours on end at her room at the Sheraton, then taken to Philadelphia's City Hall, where, in front of a one-way mirror, she sat in a hard-backed chair while Brophy checked her breathing patterns, skin sensitivity, blood pressure, pulse rates—the body's telltale signs that were measured under the bombardment of thousands of questions.

There were "normal" questions interspersed with "control" questions: "Do you love your son?" "Have you told us all you know about the murder money?" "Did you ever intentionally hurt anyone?" "Did you tell us all you know about the meeting in Middlesboro, Kentucky?" "Did you ever do anything to intentionally embarrass anyone?" "Do you know who flew the money in from Washington, D.C.?" "Have you told us the entire truth about the questions asked in this test?"

Questioning like this can be excruciating. The effect on Annette Gilly, struggling to protect herself and her father—above all her father—was emotionally and physically draining. Layer after layer of her protective defenses were stripped away, and still she persisted in trying to outwit the men and the machine. As long as she could, she professed not to remember key dates, certain meetings she attended with her husband, her father's role. Day after day the tests and questioning went on, until the machine narrowed down the areas where she was concealing information.

"She just had an iron will," Brophy said. "She was able to withstand our attempts to get all the facts from her, until she finally became convinced it was her own emotions that were betraying her to the polygraph. She finally knew it was useless to hold back. She had dedicated herself to removing all of the facts of the Yablonski killings from her mind, from her conscious memory, while she was awaiting trial, but it was gradually coming back to her."

Finally, at the beginning of April 1972, Sprague, the FBI, and the Pennsylvania state police were ready to set Annette Gilly's story down on paper for her signature. It was worth the effort it took to extract. It not only doomed her already convicted husband Paul and her father Silous Huddleston—the former as a killer of Yablonski, the latter as a master plotter in the case—it also provided the first direct testimony that the United Mine Workers leadership was behind the murder of Joseph Yablonski.

Annette told of meeting with a middle-level official of the union in District 19, William Prater, a mine workers' field representative in Tennessee. She told of the involvement of Albert Pass, the secretary-treasurer of District 19, who stood several notches higher than Prater. She told of Pass's request to Washington headquarters for twenty thousand dollars to furnish Yablonski's killers. She related events of meeting after meeting whose only purpose was to discuss how to get rid of Yablonski. And she made a startling statement: "My father told me that the Yablonski murder had the approval of the 'big man.' To me that meant Tony Boyle."

In return for her complete cooperation, Annette Gilly won two promises—one expressed, the other implied. On the record went an assurance that the prosecution would not seek the death penalty in her case. This was not a difficult offer for the prosecutor to make, for as Sprague said, "The chances of getting a death penalty for a woman in Pennsylvania and getting it carried out were nil anyway." The other guarantee was never stated directly to Annette, but it was even more important to her. She was given to understand that she would never go back to prison as long as she cooperated with the prosecution. After confessing, she was transported from motels to farms to resorts, always under heavy guard and always in what was officially called "protective custody." Sprague insisted there was no deal, but she spent two months in a resort in western Pennsylvania, until embarrassing publicity about her new life as a "country gentle-woman" caused her transfer to a secret location. After her confession became public in early April 1972, Annette Gilly spent two more years cooperating in the Yablonski case, but she never again saw the inside of a prison.

Sprague needed her cooperation to keep the case moving, and he was not reluctant to defend what could be regarded as special treatment for a principal in a heinous murder case. "I've had two feelings about the participants in the Yablonski case," he said. "Those who took part in the actual shootings, you can't make deals with them because they were the actual triggermen. And at the other end of the line—the initiators—you can't make deals with the person who started it all. But for those in the conduit, there is an area for . . . arrangements. If you're inter-ested in working your way back to the beginning of a case, there you can wheel and deal with the in-between characters."

As Sprague saw it, there was another reason for compromis-ing with Annette Gilly. The case was now more than two years old, and although three accused triggermen had been brought to justice, the prosecution could have foundered. "The case against Annette Gilly in terms of what we then had as evidence was extremely weak. So was the case against her father, Hud-dleston. If anything, the case against Huddleston was weaker. Annette Gilly helped us strengthen the case against her father."

"You will never get Silous Huddleston to talk." That was what an attorney told Sprague when Huddleston was called before a grand jury in Cleveland in February 1970, six weeks after the Yablonski murders. "The death penalty doesn't scare him and he has money to hire a good lawyer."

Court testimony later showed that Huddleston's relatives were able to turn over $23,000 in cash payments to an Akron, Ohio, lawyer to defend the old man. He was sent to jail to await trial, but he was confident that a potential key witness against him would never talk—his daughter Lucy. So sitting in a jail cell in Washington County, Pennsylvania, the sixty-three-year-old man was secure in the knowledge that one day he would beat this murder rap. He had the time and he had the money.

While Annette was confessing in Philadelphia, Huddleston's lawyers made a move in Washington County Court. They requested bail for Huddleston. Sprague opposed the move, then produced Annette Gilly's confession to block any release of Huddleston from jail.

"This became a powerful cudgel against Huddleston," Sprague recalled. "You can't underestimate the effect on him of his daughter's cooperation, and her being willing to testify against her father. It is tough enough to get someone to confess to their own participation in a murder. But to get them to tell what their own father did—and be in a position to testify to that—can be devastating."

Even before Annette's confession became public, word filtered out of Philadelphia that she was talking. Huddleston heard about it and cursed her: "Lucy, you bitch, you'll be killed!"

Meanwhile, he made some oblique moves on his own behalf. First, he let it be known that he might be willing to talk to J. Edgar Hoover; that was turned down. (Hoover died a few months later.) Then Huddleston allowed that he might talk to the attorney general of the United States. But even if Richard Kleindienst had been inclined to talk to Silous Huddleston, he was having troubles of his own, with the ITT case and Senate confirmation. Rebuffed, Huddleston decided to wait for his bail hearing, but he told one of Sprague's operatives: "If I decide to cooperate with you, I will go the whole way with you."

In the back of Huddleston's scheming mind was one more reason for waiting. He had, or said he had, a promise of as much as a million dollars from the United Mine Workers, before Yablonski was killed—money that he thought would bail him out of any trouble. As long as he could, the old man held on to the wild hope that unlimited money for his defense would come through. It never did.

Huddleston was taken to court on April 13, 1972, nine days after Annette Gilly signed her confession. As a result of her statement, another arrest had just been made for the murder of Jock Yablonski. Huddleston's old friend in District 19, William Jackson Prater, a union field representative in Tennessee, was taken into custody and was being brought to Pennsylvania to face federal and state charges. Silous Huddleston sat outwardly calm in the courtroom listening to an FBI agent read Annette's twenty-two-page confession. She herself was not in court, but was at a secret location, under heavy guard.

Huddleston followed the reading of his daughter's confession on a copy in his own gnarled hands. He heard her account of his role in planning the Yablonski killing, his recruiting of his son-in-law and the other killers, his warnings to Annette not to talk. Huddleston said not a word. His application for bail was turned down, and his trial was scheduled for the following week.

Sprague was jubilant. "This confession has moved us a step up the ladder in the hierarchy of the United Mine Workers union," he said. "There will be more arrests. Our investigation is peeling it all apart."

Huddleston went back to his jail cell, and a few nights later his attorney conferred with Richard Sprague. The old man wanted to talk.

Silous Huddleston had somehow clothed himself in the role of defender of the United Mine Workers of America in District 19. He would save the union from outsiders who wanted to destroy it; in everyday conversation he came across as a perfectly normal man, until you realized that what he was talking about was murder. He could talk offhandedly about using an airplane to run down Jock Yablonski, and it made sense in the mind that was obsessed with saving District 19.

"Annette told me they were thinking of putting arsenic in Yablonski's food or cigars to kill him. Annette and I went to a store in LaFollette and bought two bottles of rat poison which had arsenic in it. We also bought three cigars and two hypodermic needles, the kind you use to vaccinate hogs. When we got home, I filled one of the hypodermic needles with water and stuck it into the cigar and squeezed the water into it. The cigar got all wet and soggy. I told Annette the rat poison would do the same thing. I told her that plan wouldn't work."

He looked harmless, with straight white hair and ordinary horn-rimmed glasses and kindly, pixieish eyes which he occasionally blinked when he didn't understand a question, especially a question from a Yankee. A kind of awkward stutter overcame his speech when he was in too great a rush to talk in his slow Tennessee accent. Annette was in awe of her father, and one can gauge how her meek husband Paul, who reluctantly became a killer, was in awe of Silous Huddleston, too. "Bill Prater and I met with Albert Pass in Middlesboro, Kentucky, and I asked Albert if it made any difference how Yablonski died. He said he didn't care, then asked why? I told him the boys had thought of using dynamite or arsenic. Albert said not to use dynamite because it would probably kill the family and only give Yablonski a headache. He said not to use arsenic because Yablonski would only get sick and the family would die. He said that the only way to kill Yablonski would be to shoot him. After that meeting, I called Paul and told him that Albert said dynamite and arsenic are out.

"I told Paul to shoot Yablonski."

Huddleston was impressed with his union leaders. At the 1968 United Mine Workers convention in Denver, he pumped the flesh of the leader, Tony Boyle, dyed black hair slicked down. That day in Denver Huddleston couldn't have been happier if he had met his Maker. He was a loyal union man and he never questioned his leaders. Only a week before the UMW election of 1969, with the murder plot in full swing in District

19, Huddleston was in the audience when Boyle declared at Madisonville, Kentucky: "Joseph Yablonski lies through his teeth! He is a hypocrite, he defames the memory and accomplishments of John L. Lewis. He talks with two tongues about democracy; on the one hand, he is claiming it doesn't exist within the UMW, and on the other running to the courts in a vicious attempt to stop the UMW election and denying eighty thousand UMW members the right to vote.

"Joseph Yablonski is guilty of a serious conflict of interest affecting the welfare of UMW members. He is guilty of a cruel hoax that seeks to turn UMW members against UMW members. He has associated himself with outsiders to try to take over the United Mine Workers. He had dragged the good name of your union through the dust by filing expensive lawsuits against the UMW. He has tried to use the courts as a forum and substitute the judgment of the courts for that of the UMW membership because he is guilty of lies, defamation of John L. Lewis, conflict of interest, and anti-union acts.

"Joseph Yablonski is unfit to be president of the United Mine Workers. He will be rejected by the membership as a power-hungry opportunist and hypocrite."

Silous Huddleston believed every one of the leader's words. Especially, he believed that Yablonski was out to destroy the votes and pensions of the retired miners, of which he was one. He did not have to be paid to knock off Yablonski. He saw it as his duty to do so:

Q. You weren't doing this for money?

A. No, sir.

Q. How much was your son-in-law, Paul Gilly, supposed to get?

A. I don't know how much he was supposed to get.

Q. Never discussed that?

A. He was to get the fifteen thousand dollars; that was up to him about what he done with it.

Q. And you weren't interested in the money at all?

A. No, not at all.

Q. You were doing this for the good of the union?

A. Yes, sir.

Q. What was Jock Yablonski's campaign position that you disagreed with so much?

A. I didn't disagree with his campaign position so much, it was other things.

Q. Well, tell us what you disagreed with about Jock Yablonski that justified your killing the man?

A. The thing that, well, brought up that he filed a case in court, in federal court, to dismiss all pensioners out of the union, which automatically disqualified them for a pension or for a hospital card.

Q. Where did he file that case?

A. I don't know. He said in federal court.

Q. Who said?

A. Albert Pass, and William Prater, both, told me in federal court.

Q. Who represented the United Mine Workers in that case, do you know?

A. I don't know who represented them, whoever was their attorneys up there. They said the federal judge eventually ruled against them. He took it to the court of appeals, federal court of appeals.

Q. And you felt our courts weren't suited to decide disputes and you wanted him killed? The case that you say Prater and Pass told you about related to pension rights, is that right, pension rights of miners?

A. It related to dismissing all pensioners out of the union, which automatically canceled their pension and their hospitalization.

Q. That was your understanding of the suit that Prater and Pass told you about, is that right?

A. That's right. . . . They told me that was the suit that was filed in federal court. . . .

I decided, they asked me to find somebody to do the job for

them. I asked these boys if he thought he could find them. He said he could. I told them he found them. That was it.

Q. Now, you mentioned something about Mr. Pass saying that there was a particular financial backing for Mr. Yablonski in connection with his candidacy for the union presidency?

A. Yes, he said Continental Oil was backing him.

Q. Mr. Pass told you that Continental Oil was backing Mr. Yablonski?

A. Yes, sir.

Q. Does Continental Oil operate out of Kentucky or Tennessee?

A. They own coal lands all over the nation or practically all over, what don't belong to the steel companies. . . .

Q. After Mr. Pass told you, did you check that out in any way to see if that was true?

A. I had no way of checking that out. I ain't got that kind of money. . . .

Q. You're the kind of fellow that believes your leaders, is that right?

A. Yes, sir. If you don't follow your leader, what use have you got for people?

Q. And the leaders you don't believe, you've killed, is that right?

A. I've never killed any of them.

Q. You didn't?

A. No, sir.

On May 3, 1972, Silous Huddleston hobbled slowly on the arm of a sheriff into the Washington County Court. He was carrying an oxygen device, to relieve his respiratory ailments. He sat down gingerly before the bar of the court and then entered a plea of guilty to three counts of murder in the Yablonski case.

"And you are admitting a conspiracy with others?" Sprague asked.

"Yes, sir."

"And did you arrange and cause those deaths?"

"Yes."

Less than an hour later, Silous Huddleston, who "never saw a nickel" of the million dollars he said United Mine Workers promised in case of trouble, was led out of the courtroom. And the Yablonski murder case entered a new phase.

7

The Chain of Command

IN THE HILLS and coal fields of eastern Tennessee, the persistence of a bald, pipe-smoking FBI agent named Henry A. Quinn, Jr., was beginning to pay off. Quinn had spent many weeks trying to get twenty-three elderly miners to tell what they knew about the Joseph Yablonski murder case. He ranged over large parts of District 19 of the UMW, but found at first that the men didn't want to talk to him. They weren't particularly interested in talking to an outsider, and they especially didn't want to talk to a lawman. Henry Quinn played down his FBI role. When he went around to talk to the old guys like David Brandenburg, a septuagenarian fundamentalist preacher who was the secretary-treasurer of Huddleston's UMW local, Quinn would spend hours talking about the crops, the weather, or what it was like in the coal mines years ago. Every so often Quinn slipped in a word or two about that Yablonski murder investigation up north, just to let Brandenburg and the other miners know he was still a lawman. But the main thing was to get the confidence of the pensioned miners.

In Washington, D.C., at the Justice Department, work on the case was also paying off for a tall, red-haired Alabaman named Tom Henderson. One of a flock of young lawyers who entered the Justice Department during the Robert Kennedy era, he stayed on through the first Nixon administration and developed a special competence for the Yablonski case. Henderson assisted in the prosecution of Tony Boyle for the illegal union political contributions of 1968. While Annette Gilly was confessing in Philadelphia, Boyle was being found guilty of the political donations.

And in Philadelphia, the special prosecutor was masterminding the overall scenario of the case that had now been pushed to a new level by the confessions of Annette and Huddleston. William Prater had been arrested as a result of the woman's statement, and Huddleston's confession led to the arrest of another District 19 official, Albert Pass. Sprague was in no hurry, for he viewed all the efforts as leading to an inevitable conclusion.

The work in Tennessee was crucial. The retired miners were still as loyal to the union and Tony Boyle as they had been when they were active coal miners. In the structure of the union, the pensioners had full voting rights, and sometimes they were employed on organizing missions, despite their retirement. But when they were called before grand juries in Cleveland and Kentucky that were investigating the Yablonski murders and the source of the murder money, they said to a man that they knew nothing about the murders, that the money they received was for union-organizing purposes. Six union field representatives, including Prater, backed them up.

Agent Quinn was perfectly cast for his part. He was more than the usual low-key FBI man; he was downright home folks. His face was round and pink-cheeked, topped by spectacles and a balding pate graying at the temples. When he put his pipe in his mouth, he looked like a kindly uncle. Then there was his accent. Though he was born in South Carolina, Henry Quinn had worked in Tennessee for more than twenty-five years. He had the slow easy drawl and polite manners of the Tennessee hill people, and he even used their colloquialisms. He knew how to refer to years as southern miners did—"19 and 69"—he knew what a "poke salad" was.

Quinn also learned subtle touches of psychology in dealing with the old miners in District 19. Though his conversations with them were informal, he never adopted their casual manner of dress—checked shirts, bib overalls, and heavy boots. Quinn never discarded his tie or jacket, though he occasionally wore a sport coat when he went to visit the men.

"I wanted to preserve the original image these men had of me," Quinn said. "Once these people get an impression of you, they like you to live up to it. I didn't want to destroy that."

In the spring of 1972, the FBI out of Knoxville heard reports that some of the elderly miners might be in a talking frame of mind. From the north, reports were filtering down to District 19 that Annette Gilly was talking and that her father might do the same. At least two officials of District 19 were going to be arrested in the Yablonski case, the reports said, and if that was true, other arrests might follow.

One day, talking with David Brandenburg, who had been Huddleston's secretary-treasurer, Quinn thought he detected a change of direction in the seventy-two-year-old preacher's thinking. Brandenburg asked how the case was going, and Quinn, laying on his southern accent thicker than ever, allowed that it was going very well. It was a warm day, no kind of day to rush matters, especially in the hills of Tennessee. Quinn took a thoughtful puff on his ever-present pipe, then said to Brandenburg: "You know, Reverend, a day of reckoning is coming."

"Expect it is," said the fundamentalist preacher.

A few days later, at the invitation of the FBI, the Reverend David Brandenburg flew to Pittsburgh. Two FBI agents met him at the airport and drove him to Washington County. At the Ramada Inn he was led into a room, and there, sitting with FBI agents and Pennsylvania state policemen, was his old friend, the president of their union local, Silous Huddleston.

The two white-haired, bespectacled old men hadn't seen each other for more than two years. Huddleston had been in jails all that time, awaiting trial in the Yablonski murders. A lot had happened since their last meeting—Boyle's victory over

Yablonski, Yablonski's murder, and now the Miners for Democracy had just won a court-ordered rerun of the 1969 election. Things were changing in District 19 and the United Mine
Workers, and in the back of Brandenburg's mind was the
knowledge that he had handled eight thousand dollars in cash
for Huddleston—"blood money," it was later called.

Huddleston, breathing deeply on his oxygen device to relieve
his congested lungs, opened his eyes wide and said, "Dave, I've
told all I know to these fellas. I've told the truth. And I want
you and the boys back home to do the same. Tell them to do
likewise, or you'll be facing a murder charge yourself."

Brandenburg was silent, disbelief creeping over his wrinkled
face. He examined the garish red furnishings in the motel room
and he looked outside the window at the sunshine afternoon.
"I reckon so," the Reverend Brandenburg said at last. "The
truth . . ."

The next day he went up to Pittsburgh, thirty miles away,
and talked to his third federal grand jury.

Huddleston's confession brought about the arrest of the
most feared man among the coal miners in District 19, Albert
Pass, the secretary-treasurer of the district, who operated out
of Middlesboro, Kentucky, near the Tennessee line. Pass's arrest in Kentucky and transfer to Pennsylvania made David
Brandenburg's job easier back home. In the minds of the retired
coal miners, who depended so much on the orders and whims
of their union leaders, the fear of the union was beginning to
dissolve.

The followers of Silous Huddleston and David Brandenburg
were afraid of Pass because of the power he wielded on behalf
of international headquarters in Washington. Pass was an international executive board member for another district, in
Alabama, and could walk in unannounced and see Tony Boyle
any time he wished. Pass's power went vertically from District
19 President William Turnblazer to field representatives like
William Prater, and now Prater and Pass were under arrest in

the Yablonski killings, and Turnblazer was being questioned intensely by the FBI in Knoxville. The retired miners often saw Prater, seldom saw the other officials, but they knew whom Prater was speaking for when he enunciated union policy. They liked Prater, a chunky, red-faced man in his early fifties who was smooth of manner and courtly in demeanor, always helpful with pension and hospital problems.

Now after the arrest of Prater and Pass, word came back to Tom Henderson in the Justice Department: Brandenburg's "boys," who had feared Albert Pass for so long, were no longer afraid. Although they had told two federal grand juries about money they received from the union in 1969, they were now willing to change their stories. Who were they? Frail old men like Bronce Waldroop, who could hardly speak; Billy Lowe, who signed his name with an X; Harvey Huddleston (no relation to Silous), who had worked in the mines of Tennessee for fifty-five years and had recently undergone an operation for a brain tumor; and two field representatives named Corwin Edwin Ross and George Washington Hall, who was hard of hearing and who had been afraid, too. The twenty-three retired men were now saying they never received the money they were supposed to for union organizing. They had received forty-six checks, two each, and kicked the money back to field representatives like Bill Prater. In Washington, Tom Henderson perked up when he heard about the new stories the old men were telling. It wasn't clear just where the money went after it left Prater's hands, but now it was going to be easier to find out.

The union called it the "Research and Information Committee." The money totaled $19,970, and according to the union's story the twenty-three miners were given the money for union work between the fall of 1968 and the spring of 1969.

But there were holes in the story. First, there was no union organizing to be shown for the money. If the union expended the money to recruit new members in District 19, there wasn't a single new union card to show for it. And it was unclear when the expense vouchers were drawn up. Burrowing through a mass of union records, government agents finally pinpointed a date when the vouchers were prepared—February 1970, nearly two months after the Yablonski murders.

Did the old men get the union money for unfruitful organizing efforts? The vouchers showed the dates on which they were supposed to be out organizing, but again there were inconsistencies. Harvey Huddleston, who received money for organizing work supposedly performed in October 1968, was actually in the hospital then, undergoing his brain operation.

In Philadelphia, Richard Sprague, collating the inconsistencies, had a term for the research and information treasury. He called it a "murder fund." And one way to clear it up was to call top union officials, including President Boyle, before a grand jury.

Boyle was summoned to a federal grand jury in Pittsburgh on May 10, 1972. He went voluntarily. He flew from Washington, D.C., along with the UMW general counsel, Edward L. Carey; his personal attorney, Plato Cacheris; and other union officers, including District 19 President William Turnblazer, whose associates Prater and Pass had recently been arrested in the Yablonski case. Turnblazer was the most nervous of the group, because the federal agents were zeroing in on District 19 and its pensioned miners. Turnblazer, a lawyer whose father had also been District 19 president, was summoned to Washington headquarters of the union the night before the grand jury appearance, and met with Boyle and the others to go over their stories about the Research and Information Committee.

Although Boyle was still president of the UMW, his tenure was under assault by the Miners for Democracy. A federal court had just overturned his 1969 reelection and ordered a new vote. Acting on the suit brought by the Department of Labor and the supporters of Jock Yablonski, Judge William B. Bryant ruled that the union had committed wholesale violations of the law's provisions for fair elections. The judge concluded that there was a "demonstrated pattern" of using union assets to insure the reelection of Boyle and his slate. The new election was to be supervised by the government.

Boyle had another problem on his mind. The Justice Department had just won a conviction against him for giving $49,000 in union money to political campaigns in 1968. It was not in itself a serious charge—many unions had done the same thing for decades, and so had many corporations. But the judge in that case had thrown the book at Boyle after learning that Boyle transferred more than $200,000 of his own assets to his wife's name on the eve of the trial. He sentenced Boyle to five years in prison and ordered him to pay fines totaling $179,000. Cacheris, the attorney who accompanied Boyle to the Pittsburgh grand jury, was taking an appeal on the conviction.

Boyle and the attorneys seemed confident when they hurried down the sixth-floor corridor at the Pittsburgh Federal Courthouse on the afternoon of May 10. There was an energetic spring in Boyle's walk. He was not a big man, but the perquisites of power had given him a certain swagger that made him seem bigger than he was.

"How're you doing?" a reporter asked him.

"Tony Boyle's doin' fine," he replied, using his accustomed third person. "Where's the action?"

A U.S. marshall pointed to the grand jury room, and Boyle disappeared inside without benefit of attorneys, who were not permitted to go in.

Two floor upstairs, coincidentally, Boyle's associate Albert Pass had just been arraigned on federal charges in connection with the Yablonski murders. If Pass knew that Boyle was coming to the courthouse that day, he didn't let on, and when his brief hearing was over, Pass was whisked back to the local lockup.

Boyle spent an hour and fifteen minutes before the grand jury. He swore that the Research and Information Committee was an idea first broached to him by Albert Pass, at the union's international convention in Denver in 1968. Boyle said Pass

Joseph "Jock" Yablonski, during his last interview, two weeks before his murder.

Claude Vealey, confessed triggerman, moments after he hit a photographer in his jail cell in Cleveland, January 1970.

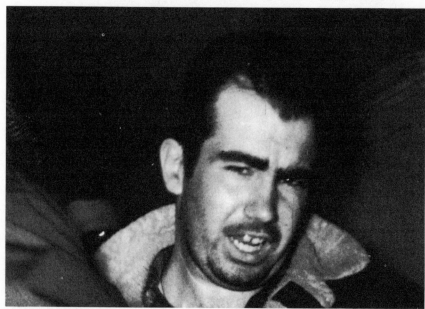

William J. Turnblazer, former president of District 19, United Mine Workers, whose testimony helped convict Tony Boyle for the Yablonski murders.

William J. Prater, former District 19 field organizer, who was convicted, then confessed his role in the murders.

Paul Gilly, triggerman who confessed a year after he was found guilty and sentenced to the electric chair.

Annette Gilly, Paul's wife, whose confession implicated her husband and father.

Silous Huddleston, father of Annette Gilly, shortly after he confessed his role in the Yablonski murders.

Albert Pass (in handcuffs), Boyle's right-hand man, displaying the grin he wore continually at his trial in Erie.

Aubran "Buddy" Martin, accompanied by Washington, Pennsylvania, authorities, at his trial where he was convicted of being one of the triggermen.

Joseph "Chip" Yablonski (left) and Kenneth Yablonski, and their wives, at the burial of their family.

Casket of Jock Yablonski is carried for burial at snow-covered Washington Cemetery.

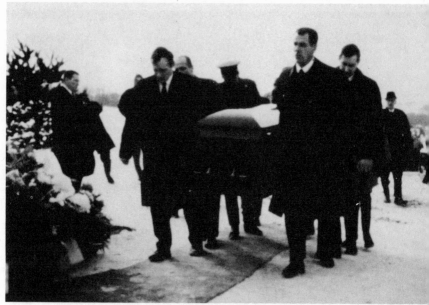

Richard A. Sprague, special prosecutor.

The Rev. David Brandenburg, Tennessee preacher and union official, leads a group of elderly miners who testified about funneling the murder-payoff money.

Arnold Miller, who succeeded Boyle as UMW president.

Tony Boyle (right) listens to his general counsel, Edward L. Carey, address supporters in Pittsburgh, three weeks before Boyle lost the 1972 election rerun.

Yablonski supporters (Miners for Democracy) protest Boyle appearance in Pittsburgh, November 1972.

Tony Boyle, three months after suicide attempt, is carried into Washington (Pennsylvania) Courthouse, December 1973, for arraignment for the three Yablonski murders.

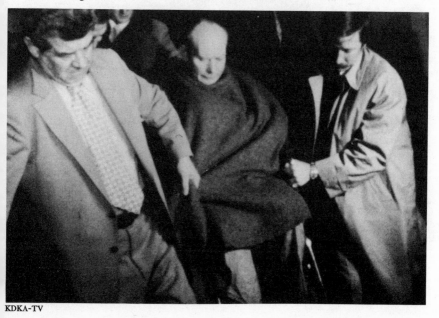

Miners for Democracy hold meeting to nominate candidates for court-ordered reelection, May 1972, Wheeling, West Virginia. On platform (left to right) Karl Kafton, Mike Trbovich, Kenneth Yablonski, and Joseph L. Rauh, Jr.

stopped him in a corridor at the convention, told how he could use elderly miners to do part-time organizing work, and said he had cleared the idea with District 19 president Turnblazer. Records from the union files were shown at the grand jury proceeding, demonstrating that the money for the organizing work was not requested until a year later, in September 1969, but Turnblazer told the grand jury he remembered how the fund was set up in Pass's conversation with Boyle at the convention.

When the grand jury session was over in late afternoon, Boyle decided not to meet with the press. His attorneys, Carey and Cacheris, went out to talk for him. Carey, a deep-voiced man who loved to quote Shakespeare, claimed to have been a coal miner himself in the hard-coal fields of eastern Pennsylvania. He was proud of that heritage, and in his capacity as general counsel of the union, he was one of the inspirations for Boyle's claim that "outsiders" were trying to take over the union. Carey bellowed that "unscrupulous people" were making "innuendos and wild statements that have no basis in fact." He left no doubt whom he meant: the special prosecutor, Richard Sprague.

Carey declared that Boyle had cooperated with the grand jury and answered every question about the Research and Information Committee. He said the nearly $20,000 in union money had been fully accounted for.

Boyle waited in another room, and when Carey and Cacheris were finished with the reporters, the three hurried back to Washington. And William Turnblazer hurried back to Tennessee to find out what David Brandenburg and the old miners were up to.

On the last weekend of May 1972, a ragtag band of nearly four hundred coal miners assembled in the field house of Wheeling College, a liberal Catholic school in Wheeling, West Virginia. The skies were sunny, and the miners, cheered by the spring weather, were optimistic. In terms of numbers, they

represented only a fraction of the 200,000 members of the
United Mine Workers of America. But in terms of the future
of their embattled union, they represented an historic milestone.
This was the first rank-and-file convention in the history of
organized labor. Never before had a breakaway movement gone
so far within the structure of a major labor union in the United
States.

"Bullets cannot kill an idea," said one of the delegates.

They called themselves Miners for Democracy. They knew
little about Robert's Rules of Order, parliamentary procedure,
or writing a constitution. But they knew what they wanted.
They showed that when Ken and Chip Yablonski got up to greet
them. The field house rocked with their thundering applause
and foot-stamping cheers.

The temporary chairman of the meeting, Karl Kafton, had
come a long way since the day of Jock Yablonski's funeral.
Then, he had been afraid to sign a legal paper to continue Jock's
court fight, saying simply, "I'm scared." Now Kafton made a
joke he never would have attempted three years earlier—he
suggested that the accordionist play "Montana." The convention roared. The delegates did not have to be told whose home
state that was—Tony Boyle's. "I'm told if they don't play 'Montana' the band won't get paid," said Kafton. More derisive
laughter. The delegates also didn't have to be reminded that
Boyle's forces spent $200,000 on bands at the 1964 international
convention in Miami.

When the joking and cheering died down, the Miners for
Democracy wrote a kind of Diet of Worms attack on the incumbent leadership of the United Mine Workers. They approved
a thirty-four-point platform that ran the gamut from such radical ideas as cutting officers' salaries to moving the union headquarters out of Washington and into the coal fields. They called
for a strong, union-led safety program—coal would be mined
safely or not at all, they said. The days of fatalism in the coal
mines were over.

Three men wanted the nomination for president—Arnold

Miller, Harry Patrick, and Mike Trbovich. Miller and Patrick were from West Virginia, and Trbovich had been a neighbor and campaign manager of Jock Yablonski's. As the delegates balloted, Patrick withdrew from the race, then Miller beat Trbovich by a narrow margin. In a show of unity, the Miners for Democracy then named Trbovich as the candidate for vice president and Patrick for secretary-treasurer.

The new organization said it would need $60,000 to win control of the union from the forces of Tony Boyle—the same amount Yablonski spent on his campaign in 1969. They were confident they could raise it among dissident miners who had been exploited for so long by their union bosses.

On the red-white-and-blue-bedecked platform of the fieldhouse where the Miners for Democracy held their historic meeting, there was a picture of Jock Yablonski, hands outstretched, standing in front of a statue of John Mitchell, a turn-of-the-century president of the United Mine Workers. Nearby was a quote from Yablonski: "It's time someone spoke up regardless of what the sacrifice may be."

To thunderous applause, Chip Yablonski told the delegates they'd come a long way since 1969. "Tony Boyle and his crowd have been indicted and convicted," Chip declared, "and there's more to come and you know it!"

Ken Yablonski, his thin lips set in a determined scowl, attacked "those vicious, filthy, demented-minded people that have wrested control of this union away from the men.

"They thought they were going to end it when they murdered my mother and my sister and my father," Ken Yablonski said. "But you didn't let them end it. On December tenth, in the early-morning hours, when we saw the votes being rolled up against us, my dad said, 'I never lost an election in the United Mine Workers, and I never lost this one. They stole it from me. I'm going to prove that this was the crookedest election in the history of the labor movement.' "

Joseph Rauh, Yablonski's lawyer who had done so much before and after Yablonski's death to shake the union establishment, watched the proceedings happily. The miners were on the march, Rauh said, and nothing could stop them. Remembering the corruption and payroll-padding and violence of the 1969 election campaign, Rauh told the Miners for Democracy: "There is no doubt in either my head or my heart that we will win this struggle. The days of Tony Boyle and his whole corrupt crowd are numbered. Yes, Tony, the walls of justice are closing in on you."

8

Rerun

Delegate Marion Ladisic: Take that shit-eating grin off of your face, or somebody will wipe it off for you! Do you hear? Somebody will wipe it off your face. We are through being polite to you.

Chairman Mike Budzanoski: Sit down.

Delegate Steve Kovich: What do you mean, sit down? What the hell is this "sit down"?

Chairman Budzanoski: Brother Vince Zmuda has the floor.

Delegate Zmuda: I will wait.

Delegate Ladisic: Because you have these people all over the hall, you have these people bought off, and you can do whatever you want.

Chairman Budzanoski: You do not have the floor.

Delegate Ladisic: I got the floor! I am taking the floor! What are you going to do about it? I am taking the floor. What are you going to do about it?

Delegate Kovich: Let him have it!

Delegate Ladisic: I am taking the floor! What are you going to do about it? What are you going to do about it?

Chairman Budzanoski: Sit down, Brother Ladisic.

Delegate Ladisic: You make me sit down!

Delegate Karpoff: This is democracy? . . .

Delegate Harry Rossi: I am tired of this goddam bullshit. We aren't doing a thing here but raising hell. I move we adjourn now.

Meetings of the United Mine Workers at the district level often descended into fist-waving shouting matches, but the chaos at the meeting of District 5 in May 1970 was a forerunner of change to come. It happened four months after the bodies of Jock Yablonski and his wife and daughter were found at their home, and the struggle for power in Jock's old district—against his sucessor as district president, Budzanoski—was a clear indication that the days of the Tony Boyle regime were numbered.

At stake was more than the rebirth of the movement led by Yablonski. Marion Ladisic and his small band of Miners for Democracy were reaching for the mantle of John L. Lewis.

The United Mine Workers of America was founded in 1890. For more than half its history it was dominated by the awesome figure of Lewis. Often called a patriarch, he was in fact a dictator, who set the union's policy and tolerated no opposition. He led the union into and then out of the mainstream of American labor. Even after he stepped down as president of the Mine Workers in 1960, he continued to exert his powerful influence until the day he died in 1969. Even in death, he had a hand in the course his union took.

Lewis's death on June 11, 1969, gave Tony Boyle a chance to expand his own power, then being shaken by the three-week-old candidacy of Jock Yablonski. By a fast sleight of hand, Boyle had himself appointed as Lewis's successor on the union's rich Welfare and Retirement Fund. Besides insuring most of the votes of the pensioned miners, whose monthly stipends Boyle proceeded to raise to $150, his power over the pension and hospital cards was a clear message to old miners in places like Tennessee and Kentucky. They knew their pensions or hospital bills could be cut off if they didn't help reelect President Boyle.

Boyle was able to engineer capers like that in 1969 because he was the autocrat of the union. But by 1972 things were different. The union election was now being rerun, and the federal government was policing the campaign and the election.

It was an unprecedented situation in American labor. Not only were Boyle and his henchmen under court order not to

spend union money for reelection purposes, but they couldn't
even campaign on union time. They had to go out on weekends,
at their own expense, if they were to reach the voting miners.
And federal agents and volunteer observers from other unions
were on hand to make sure they complied.

Moreover, Boyle could no longer use the UMW *Journal* as
his personal house organ. In 1969, Boyle was able to exclude
mention of Yablonski's candidacy for five months. In 1972, the
Miners for Democracy were given equal advertising space in the
pages of the *Journal* for the duration of the election campaign.
Now, instead of the former unbridled praise for W. A. "Tony"
Boyle, coal miners were reading about the endorsement of Arnold Miller by a close associate of John L. Lewis, Josephine
Roche. Miss Roche, then eighty-six years old, was a former
assistant secretary of the treasury and was the woman whose
proxy vote Boyle claimed to have when he took control of the
Welfare and Retirement Fund. She gave one thousand dollars
to Arnold Miller's campaign, and in a statement published in
the union *Journal,* she told the union's coal miners:

"Just before his death, Mr. Lewis confided to me that his
deepest concern was that W. A. "Tony" Boyle would destroy
the Welfare Fund just as he was destroying the union. We talked
on numerous occasions about this during those final months and
his major concern was how to protect the Fund. . . .

"What John L. Lewis built is today being destroyed. Mr.
Lewis was ill in 1969 and died shortly after Joseph Yablonski
announced his candidacy for the UMW presidency. Had Mr.
Lewis lived he would not have been neutral. He would have
supported Jock Yablonski with all his vigor. Jock's courage and
determination live on through Miners for Democracy."

Arnold Miller, a simple man from West Virginia who had
been a coal miner as recently as 1970, had a simple campaign:
He was going to restore democracy to the United Mine Workers. He was a plain-speaking man, his wavy silver hair making
him look older that his fifty-one years. He was partially disabled,
suffering from black lung disease, and had a withered left ear,

a reminder of his active duty in Europe during the Second World War. Miller ranged up and down the coal fields in 1972, to places where Jock Yablonski had been afraid to campaign, and took his message: "This union is going to be run by its rank and file."

For the United Mine Workers, it was a radical message. No one dared preach it while John L. Lewis was alive. Coal miners had developed a fatalism about their lives. Accident or death was a daily prospect that had to be faced, and the leaders of the union knew best.

Their fatalism was expressed at union conventions. The international union meets every four years, and by the time of the 1968 convention, the power of Tony Boyle was absolute and unquestioned. Lyndon Johnson sent his "warmest personal greetings" to President Boyle, and Vice President Hubert Humphrey gave his first speech to a labor union as the newly chosen Democratic candidate for president. Addressing Boyle as "Tony, the one and only Tony Boyle," Humphrey told the delegates how lucky they were to have such great leadership come from their ranks. Boyle's power was so pervasive that an international board member, Jock Yablonski, was moved to get up and tell the assemblage:

"I am happy to be here and I lack the words which would enable me to describe the love, the devotion and the respect for the integrity of every member of our union that our distinguished president has. He has a continuous concern for our welfare. He does great work not only in his office but before the governmental agencies and down in the White House. Every night when he leaves late, he takes with him volumes of work to be completed before the next morning's business. . . .

"With a leader like this, with a leader with this kind of devotion, with a leader who tells it like it is, loud and clear, and with a leader who stays right in the middle of where the action is, this union can never go too far wrong. . . . It is, indeed, a great privilege and a pleasure for me to present to you my very good friend, President Tony Boyle."

A "spontaneous" demonstration, thirty minutes or more in length, followed.

Yablonski's son Kenneth also genuflected before President Boyle at the 1968 convention. He praised Boyle for his help in winning compensation for widows of a mine disaster in Pennsylvania. The case took six years to settle, out of court, for a quarter of a million dollars.

Ken Yablonski told the convention, "I listened to President Boyle asking question after question of the officials of the United States Steel Corporation, and many a time they didn't want to answer, because they knew what he was getting at, and I couldn't help but think that something was happening there, and the person that we felt most obligated to, and that the widows felt most obligated to, was President Boyle."

The conventioners pressed Boyle to accept a raise in salary, or at least an expensive present. President Boyle refused, and up rose Jock Yablonski again.

"Now, what are you going to do for this fellow?" Yablonski said. "He won't accept an increase in salary; he won't accept a gift from his fellow officers; and I guess about the only thing that we can do is to really try to the utmost of our ability to provide the real honest-to-God, loyal support for him and his administration that they deserve."

So even Jock Yablonski was not immune to the slavish worship of union leaders. As Ken Yablonski put it several years later: "It was more than just 'going along to get along.' You wouldn't be in the union unless you kissed Boyle's ass. You might not even have your head intact if you incurred his disfavor." Far from being embarrassed by his own and his father's words at the 1968 convention, Ken Yablonski today points to that time as the highwater mark of the union dictatorship.

All that began to change soon after the Yablonski murders. When delegate Marion Ladisic stood up in 1970 and told District 5 president Mike Budzanoski what to do with the grin on his face, it was only four months since Jock Yablonski had been buried, but a new spirit was already sweeping the union. At district after district, rank-and-file miners were sending out the word that, like Jock Yablonski, they would no longer submit to the discipline of Tony Boyle and his cohorts.

In this, Ladisic and his rebels in the Miners for Democracy were following in the tradition of John L. Lewis. Though he dictated union policy, Lewis had what Boyle could never achieve—the courage and strength to stand up for what he believed in when he felt that his union was threatened. Boyle hired public relations men and tried to use union funds to enshrine him and preserve his power, but Lewis fought with his fists and his fiery mouth. Boyle cozied up to coal operators and wanted to be a part of the labor-union establishment, but Lewis showed equal disdain for labor bosses, company presidents, the Supreme Court, and several presidents of the United States. When, in 1947, the Taft-Hartley Act was passed with a requirement for non-Communist oaths by union leaders, Lewis angrily confronted the American Federation of Labor executive board. He demanded that labor not give in to the oath, but the forces of AFL President George Meany overpowered him. The UMW leader unloaded his most biting vitriol to denounce the AFL—"lions led by asses," he called the establishment—but he lost. And he led his union out of the House of Labor forever.

The rerun of the election Jock Yablonski lost was conducted under the tightest outside supervision in the history of the American labor movement. About one thousand federal agents policed the campaign, which ran from July to December 1972. Labor Department officials monitored the union's Washington headquarters, its books, its district officials, its expenditure of every penny.

While Boyle sat brooding during weekdays in his Washington office, forbidden to make any political trips to the coal fields on union time, Miller, Trbovich, and Patrick carried the Miners for Democracy drive to thousands of union men in Pennsylvania, West Virginia, Tennessee, Kentucky, Illinois—to places where Jock Yablonski was loved and to places where he feared to go.

Boyle lashed out at the MFD as the "stooges" for outsiders. Incongruously, he saw them as the agents both of Communists and nonunion coal companies. He charged that sinister "foundations" were putting up the money for the "three stooges." The "gang of outsiders," he said, were front men for those who would destroy the union.

Oddly enough, Boyle never went near a coal mine during the six-month campaign. He spoke at rallies and dinners, some of them embarrassing. At Grundy, Virginia, he used his Labor Day holiday to star in a rally billed in advance as attracting 10,000 supporters. Some observers said only 2000 persons showed up, the Boyle faction claimed that the turnout was around 4000. But whatever the exact attendance that day, the absentees included the governor of West Virginia, a senator from Virginia, and a congressman from Kentucky. All three had been invited to the Boyle rally but had found other things to do that Labor Day.

Arnold Miller was no soapbox orator, but his unpretentious message, spoken without histrionics, reached the coal miners of the nation. He spoke of bread-and-butter issues.

"Tony Boyle backs the management," said the Miners for Democracy. "Arnold Miller backs the man." The rebels charged that Boyle was in bed with the coal operators. He had signed a "secret contract" with the nation's two largest coal companies and a number of smaller companies. In return, the companies could pay only twenty cents a ton royalty at certain mines, instead of the specified forty cents in the contract. That deal, said Miller's people, cost the union's welfare fund more than fifteen million dollars in uncollected royalties.

"Every day, coal operators break our contract," said Miller. "Every day, they violate our seniority rights. Every day, the companies fire good union men without cause. Why? Because the operators know that when a grievance case reaches the district level, Boyle's stooges will sell us out. The only way we can fight for our contract rights under Boyle is to sacrifice our wages and strike. It's time to stop romancing the companies."

To the charges that they were dominated by "outsiders" or Communists, the MFD campaigners replied that John L. Lewis, too, had been called an outsider and a communist.

"They called him a Communist and a radical," the MFD declared. "They said John L. Lewis would break the union and betray the rank-and-file. It's one of the oldest union-busting tactics known. It's called the Big Lie. And they're using it again. . . . A lot of people have grown wealthy off the UMW and the Welfare Fund. They know that when the Miller ticket is elected, the gravy train ends.

"A lot of people get fat salaries from the union for doing nothing. They know they'll be out of work when the rank-and-file elects its own district officials.

"A lot of people have led the easy life by making deals with the coal operators. They know that with the Miller ticket leading the UMWA, the deals—and the easy life—are over."

In one last desperate push late in the campaign, Boyle carried his drive to West Virginia and Pennsylvania, on weekend forays to speak to what was left of his loyalists. Accompanying him was his outspoken general counsel, Edward L. Carey. In Pittsburgh on a Sunday in November, they met with Boyle supporters at a downtown hotel, and Boyle and Carey spoke for two hours. MFD pickets surrounded the hotel, marching under banners, signs, and upraised fists. "Arrest Boyle for Murder," one of the signs proclaimed. Boyle managed to avoid seeing them, and in the basement of the hotel he cheerfully greeted a group of miners who had paid twenty dollars each for the privilege of attending the "testimonial." Numerous pro-Boyle officials of the union were there from District 5, but since they were prohibited by government order from contributing to the election campaign, they had to buy their own luncheons. In protest, they carried lunch pails to the hotel dining room.

The Boyle supporters had expected about five hundred to

show up for the luncheon. Fewer than three hundred attended, and about one hundred of these were payrollers and pensioners who had been transported to the hotel. It was a far cry from the days when thousands of miners had thronged the very same hotel to hear Boyle speak about the greatness of the union.

"Stooges!" Boyle cried out at the luncheon. "Outsiders! They want to control and destroy this union! Your president is being attacked because he's been too militant on behalf of your union."

And Edward Carey, haranguing the audience with an old-fashioned, give-em-hell speech, deplored the campaign against the Boyle leadership, and came up with the nonsequitur of the day: "Forgive them, Father, for they know not what they do."

The new election was held during the first eight days of December 1972. This time, the government counted the votes. Because polling places were widely dispersed across the nation's coal fields, it took a week to tally all the ballots. But on December 16, the result was unmistakable. Although almost the same number of miners had cast ballots as in 1969, this time Tony Boyle was finished, beaten by the Arnold Miller ticket by a decisive count of 70,373 to 56,334. Two days later, at a meeting of the union's international executive board in New York, W. A. "Tony" Boyle resigned as president of the United Mine Workers of America.

Before the year was out, Miller and his followers took over the former private club at 900 Fifteenth Street in Washington that had been the union's headquarters for more than thirty years. One of their first acts was to remove an iron gate at the main stairway inside that had literally sealed off the rank and file from its leaders. Then Miller's reformers auctioned off the Cadillac limousines that had been used by Boyle and his fellow officers, conducting the auction among coal miners. Chip Yablonski was installed as general counsel of the union, at a salary $10,000 a year less than Edward Carey had received, and Miller and the other new officers also reduced their pay. Finally, Miller's administration fired the entire twenty-three-member international executive board that had performed so loyally for Tony Boyle. Thenceforth, all its members would be elected by the rank and file.

Boyle retired to his home in Georgetown, suffering another disgrace in having his full-salary pension of $50,000 a year cut back to $16,000. He vaguely considered a legal challenge to the union election, but he knew he was finished as a labor leader. He had just turned seventy-one, and hanging over his head was a five-year sentence for violating the Corrupt Practices Act, a conviction that was still on appeal.

Boyle's future was still uncertain when, shortly after the new year began, he received a telephone call from a lawyer. How would he like to testify for the defense at another Yablonski murder trial, in Erie, Pennsylvania?

9

The Heavy Artillery

WHEN *Commonwealth of Pennsylvania* vs. *William Jackson Prater* went to trial at the Erie County Courthouse in March 1973, the contrast with previous legal actions in the Joseph Yablonski murder case could not have been more pointed.

There was the defendant Prater—the sixth person to be charged with the Yablonski murders, and the first full-time official of the United Mine Workers to be accused. Prater was a District 19 field representative in Tennessee, a seemingly respectable man of fifty-three, with seven children and no prior arrest record. At the time he went on trial he was the highest official of the union to be charged with the murders; and at Erie the prosecution transformed him into a surrogate defendant for Tony Boyle.

There was the judge, Edward H. Carney, a veteran of ten years on the Erie bench, a former FBI man. Unlike Judge Charles Sweet, who had presided over the Yablonski murder cases in Washington County, Judge Carney made himself almost invisible during Prater's trial; he was not overbearing, nor did he make wisecracks. He was trying the case because the Pennsylvania Supreme Court, at the behest of attorneys for Prater and Albert Pass, had ordered the cases transferred out of Washington County. To insure a dignified atmosphere, Judge Carney ordered the courtroom and courthouse surrounded by state police and sheriff's deputies, with orders to allow no one to enter or leave the courtroom during Prater's trial.

There was the courthouse. Unlike Washington County's rococo edifice, where previous trials in the murders had been held, the Erie courthouse was a classic pre-Civil War structure of gray stone. Its huge Courtroom Number One resembled a church, dominated by a greatly enlarged replica of the Commonwealth of Pennsylvania Seal—"Virtue, Liberty, Independence."

And finally, there was the special prosecutor from Philadelphia. Richard Sprague had been moonlighting for more than three years in the Yablonski case, but now for the first time he was going to try to prove that the United Mine Workers was behind the killing of the rebel Yablonski. Sprague planned on a long trial—three weeks, he estimated. For the defense, there would be not only Prater on the witness stand, but Aubran Martin, the convicted killer; Albert Pass, Boyle's associate who was awaiting trial; and Boyle himself. Sprague dug in at the Holiday Inn in downtown Erie with a small battalion of assistants, police, and witnesses. One of Sprague's assistants noted, "This will be the Maginot Line of the case. They're bringing in the heavy artillery. But we'll have a few bombshells of our own."

On the evening of Tuesday, March 6, with the Prater jury still being chosen, a chartered bus from the Erie airport rolled in to the Holiday Inn in downtown Erie. On hand as a sort of shepherd was Sprague's Detective Sergeant Robert Winchester. It was after ten in the evening, but the aged, travel-weary men, nineteen in all, who stepped into the motel lobby seemed bright and cheerful. Some of them were hard of hearing. Some wore bib overalls. One was in a wheelchair. Another had had brain surgery. The men, most of them in their seventies, seemed innocently curious, even bewildered. For many of them, it was their first trip outside Tennessee in their entire lives. These were the retired coal miners—one had worked for fifty-five years in the mines of Appalachia. They were in Erie to testify against William Jackson Prater, a man they knew well. The group constituted the "Research and Information Committee" the union set up in the late summer of 1969 to receive $20,000 from union headquarters in Washington.

"Gosh darn," said their leader, David Brandenburg, "sure is cold up here."

Brandenburg was a "holiness preacher" from LaFollette, Tennessee, Prater's home town, and an officer of a coal miners union local made up of pensioned men. Brandenburg's hobby was collecting, and playing with, snakes, which his fundamentalist beliefs told him could cause him no harm.* He was in his midseventies, his second wife was fifty years younger, and they had a three-year-old baby daughter.

But Brandenburg was more than a pious preacher—according to earlier testimony in the case, he had held Yablonski murder money in his hands. He had denied knowing anything about the murders, and before two grand juries, he had defended the United Mine Workers Union. Now Brandenburg was in Erie to tell, on the witness stand, where the money came from. He was leading his "boys" to a "day of reckoning." And he was eager to play a major role in the outcome of his friend Prater's trial.

Immediately upon arriving at the Holiday Inn in Erie, Pennsylvania, Brandenburg and his cohorts began meeting with Sprague to mesh their stories about the committee. "All we want to do is tell the truth, boys," Brandenburg said at one prep session with Sprague.

In Pennsylvania, prosecution and defense are permitted to make opening summary statements to the jury. Sprague used this occasion to generate more headlines in the case and to make an impact on the jury before it retired for the weekend. Defense attorney H. David Rothman declined his option.

"Blood money" was the way Sprague described the research

---

* "Behold, I give unto you power to tread on serpents and scorpions, and over all the power of the enemy: and nothing shall by any means hurt you." Luke 10:19

and information fund when he addressed the completed jury three days after Brandenburg's arrival. "This money was taken from the sweat and work of other miners to kill a fellow miner."

On this occasion, too, for the first time in a court of law, Sprague proposed a direct connection between Tony Boyle and the Yablonski murders.

"This is what this case is all about; the assassination of a family," said Sprague. "We are going back to the beginning, step by step."

He called William Prater "a conduit along the way." He said that a higher union official, Albert Pass, made an unusual request of Tony Boyle in the summer of 1969—authorization for $10,000 to be spent in the union's District 19, in Tennessee and Kentucky.

"You will see the checks on which that money was transferred," Sprague promised the jury. "You gonna hear how there was a second letter asking for ten thousand dollars more. And you're gonna hear how just before Thanksgiving, Prater told Silous Huddleston: 'Boyle's gonna wait, hold up on the murder,' and how Huddleston told his people, 'Hold up.'

"And then you're gonna hear how, with the election apparently won by Boyle, Prater went back to Huddleston and said, 'Go ahead, get it done, but get it done before the first of the year.'"

Sprague would up by saying that he would prove Prater guilty of murder in the first degree, but he scarcely mentioned Prater in his address. In his remarks about going back to the beginning, Sprague took the case closer to the door of Tony Boyle. Sprague knew that Boyle would come to Erie and testify in Prater's defense.

Judge Carney imposed strict security instructions for the proceedings. Spectators were searched with electronic equipment before entering the courtroom. No one could enter or leave during court sessions.

As soon as there was a recess, the reporters hurried to their telephones to spread the news of Sprague's reference to Boyle.

By that afternoon, another denial of any knowledge of the murders was coming out of Washington from William Anthony Boyle, recently retired miner.

Even as Boyle's newest denial was moving over the wires, Claude Edward Vealey was back on a witness stand—Vealey, whose tantalizing unexplained reference to a "man named Tony" had startled investigators three years earlier. In Erie, Vealey, now twenty-nine years old, made his third appearance as a prosecution star witness. He had helped convict Aubran Martin and he had testified against Paul Gilly a year earlier. Now, in the courtroom at Erie, Sprague was laying the groundwork for a tenuous connection between the killers and the current defendant, Prater.

"Who hired you for this job?" Sprague asked.

"Paul Gilly," said Vealey. "I told him if the money was right I would do it." He again quoted Gilly as saying "a man named Tony" was the contact man.

As the first week of the Prater trial ended, there seemed to be no connection between the three killers and Prater. Who could corroborate Vealey's story? Not Aubran Martin, who would testify for the defense. Paul Gilly? He had refused to testify at his own trial. But over that weekend, with Vealey's cross-examination held in abeyance until Monday morning, a new development helped provide the Prater connection to the murders.

Ever since Paul Gilly's trial in the late winter of 1971–72, FBI agents, at the instigation of Prosecutor Sprague, had been putting pressure on Gilly to tell what he knew about any involvement of higher-ups in the union. Gilly had steadfastly maintained his trial posture—that he was innocent and knew nothing. He made plain many times that he wasn't talking, even after his wife and her father made their confessions.

But with the Prater trial under way, pressure on Gilly came from another source—his three brothers in Indiana and Ohio. At the Western State Penitentiary in Pittsburgh, Gilly was in-

formed that his mother was stricken with cancer, and that her
dying wish was that her son should tell what he knew about the
case. Gilly began to waver.

Sprague learned that Gilly was on the brink of yielding to
the pressure. Just before the first weekend of the Prater trial,
Gerald Gold, Gilly's Cleveland lawyer, appeared at the Holiday
Inn in Erie and met with the prosecutor. Two days later, on his
way back to Erie from Philadelphia, Sprague stopped off in
Pittsburgh and, with Gold's permission, talked with Gilly at the
penitentiary. Soon Gilly was on his way to Erie, under heavy
state police guard, to make a full statement and await a courtroom appearance.

Claude Vealey, meanwhile, underwent cross-examination to
open the second week of the Prater trial. On the previous Friday, on direct examination by the prosecutor, Vealey had looked
almost respectable. Now, as defense attorney Rothman ap-
praised him in court, the jacketless Vealey looked like a thug,
in a pale blue polo shirt that exposed his bone-crushing muscles
to their awesome fullest. A uniformed deputy sheriff stood beside the confessed murderer at the witness stand.

Rothman questioned Vealey about the numerous trips he
said he made in the summer and fall of 1969, allegedly in pursuit
of Yablonski. Vealey couldn't remember certain names, but he
held firm on one point: he was hired to kill. Attorney Rothman
tried to establish that Vealey, a long-time burglar, was merely
going out on another house job, for a cache of valuables and
coins in the Yablonski home. Rothman showed that Vealey had
taken part in burglaries with Paul Gilly before, but Vealey
insisted that this one was different—it was a murder job from
the beginning. He said of Yablonski, "I was told this person
Tony had a grudge and wanted him killed."

He said that the murder was called off because of the approaching United Mine Worker election in early December,
1969. "But Gilly wanted to go ahead and get it over with,
because he had spent so much money and didn't have enough

to turn in. He had already received forty-two hundred dollars."

Defense Attorney Rothman shifted gears. He pointed out that in Vealey's 1970 signed statement to the FBI, there was nothing saying that a man named Tony wanted Yablonski killed because of a grudge.

"Who told you to say that under oath in this courtroom?" Rothman demanded.

"Nobody told me," Vealey shot back, his narrow brown eyes glistening.

"When is the first time you told anyone Gilly told you a man named Tony had a grudge?"

"The day I gave my statement," Vealey responded.

"Somebody goofed," Rothman snarled.

An objection by Sprague was sustained.

The killer agreed that he had been promised leniency, but denied being offered reward money. Then Rothman returned to the "Tony" reference. What, he asked, did the FBI want to know from Vealey about the United Mine Workers?

"I believe," said Vealey, "the only name that came up was Tony Boyle. I believe Agent [Joseph] Masterson asked me if I knew Tony Boyle."

"That's not in the statement, is it?" Rothman said contemptuously, waving the fifteen-page statement at the witness.

"No."

"Who decided what to leave in and take out?"

"I believe they did."

Rothman then brought out that Vealey was never asked by the FBI about other high union officials, that Boyle was the only union officer they asked him about.

When Vealey's cross-examination ended, Sprague attempted to have Vealey read his entire written statement into the record for the jury.

"He can't read that and he knows it!" the defense attorney shouted. The judge agreed.

Rothman delivered a final jab before Vealey left the courtroom. "You forgot to mention that [the FBI questions about

Tony Boyle] at the Aubran Martin trial?" A quick objection
by Sprague blocked the answer.

Vealey was led away, accompanied by deputy sheriffs. At
the defense table, William Prater appeared relaxed. During Vealey's hours in court, the defendant's name had never been mentioned.

It was essential for Sprague to show a direct link to Prater.
But he was less concerned about that than about continuing the
momentum he had started three years earlier, in his contention
that there was a "chain of command" in the Yablonski murders
stretching all the way up to the union leadership in Washington.

The prosecutor saw the chain of command theory this way:
In the fall of 1969, Boyle authorized two requests for money
totaling $20,000. The requests came from Albert Pass, a union
official in Appalachia and an international board member. Pass
put both requests in writing to Boyle. According to the prosecutor, the money was "covered up" by the Research and Information Committee based in the union's District 19, in Tennessee
and Kentucky. The money then went from Washington to
Prater, who broke it down into smaller checks turned over to
retired miners. They cashed the checks, kicked the money back
to union officials, and the money passed through the hands of
Silous Huddleston, in Tennessee. He channeled it through his
daughter, Annette Gilly, in Cleveland, and her husband Paul
hired the killers of Joseph Yablonski.

The checks issued to the research committee and then allegedly kicked back to union officials were to be concealed by
phony expense vouchers made up for the committee members
and signed by them. After the fact, the "blood money" was laun-
dered into legitimate union-organizing money. The courtroom
test would come when Tony Boyle, as a witness for the Prater
defense, would be questioned about the trail of the $20,000.

Paul Gilly was driven to Erie from the Western Pennsylvania Penitentiary, where he had been since his conviction a

year earlier. His three brothers wanted him to tell all he knew; their mother was dying, and it was time to clear his conscience and let her die in peace. Otherwise, the brothers told Gilly, they would never see him again. Paul Gilly decided to confess.

He was taken to Sprague's room at the Holiday Inn late on a Sunday before the second week of Prater's trial was to begin. Snow covered the ground, from Pittsburgh to Erie, and the night air was cold. Gilly shuddered in his plain black suit—the same one he had worn at his trial—as two state policemen hustled him along the third-floor balcony to Sprague's suite.

Samuel Rodgers, one of Gilly's two lawyers, was there, and so were Gilly's three brothers and a nephew. One brother in particular, William, wanted Gilly to cooperate. Bill Gilly felt the shame on the family intensely. He was determined that his brother should tell all, regardless of the consequences and without seeking a deal. But Rodgers argued that he could get Paul a better deal if he held out a little longer—maybe a reduction in the death penalty sentence to, say, twenty years.

Sprague told the Gilly brothers: "I know the shame your families have lived under these past three and a half years. I know you're basically decent people, and when you testified in Paul's trial, I did not cross-examine you and I did not question your word and your belief in your brother. I know you're probably church-going people, and quite decent people, to stick by your brother the way you have. But now's the time—it's a day of reckoning—when you, and only you, can convince Paul to do the right thing."

Sprague did make Paul Gilly one assurance—that his three life sentences would be concurrent, rather than consecutive.

Rodgers made one more attempt. "Don't talk," he argued.

Sprague said there would be no deal—it was going to be first-degree murder. William Gilly said from the other side of the room, "Talk, or we'll never see you again. If you don't talk, we'll never visit you again."

Paul Gilly turned his sad, birdlike face to Sprague and said in his quiet drawl, "I will tell the truth."

Gilly was taken to the Erie County jail, to await his testimony at Prater's trial. William turned to Sprague's assistant, William Wolf. Like Paul, he spoke slowly. "I know this is an unusual request," he told Wolf, "but me and my brothers want to speak to Joseph Yablonski, Jr. We want to tell him how sad we are and have been."

Wolf was surprised by the request, but walked down to Chip Yablonski's room and told him what had just occurred. "I know this is a difficult thing for you," he said, "but these are decent people. They want an opportunity just to get it out. Give them a break, will you? Just let them get it out."

Chip Yablonski agreed to see the Gilly brothers. He came out onto the balcony that linked the third-floor rooms, and shook hands with each of the three brothers and the nephew. Each Gilly spoke his piece about how sorry the family was that their Paul had been involved.

"I have a brother, too," the tall, serious Chip said. "If my brother had done something bad, I would have stuck by my brother. I can appreciate why you stuck by yours. I appreciate your feelings and I know you're good people."

Wolf watched it all and it was too much for him. He turned his face to the night air and wept.

The next morning, Paul Gilly took the witness stand in Courtroom Number One in Erie. For his appearance as a cooperative witness in the Yablonski case, he wore the same dark, conservative suit and narrow tie he had worn at his own murder trial a year earlier. His voice was shy, polite, almost inaudible, and cadenced in the accent of his native Kentucky. He was there to tell the third man's version of what happened the night Joseph Yablonski, his wife, and their daughter were riddled with bullets in their farmhouse.

Sprague quickly dispensed with the legal requirements. Yes, Gilly said, he had been convicted and sentenced to death on three counts of murder. (The sentences were automatically reduced to life imprisonment after the June 1972 outlawing of the death penalty by the U.S. Supreme Court.) Yes, his lawyer and family had been advised that he was testifying. Yes, he had been advised of his rights. No, he had made no deals or agreements.

"Who hired you?" Sprague asked.

"Silous Huddleston and my wife Annette," said Gilly. He said that sometime in August 1969, he became aware that his wife and father-in-law had "made an agreement with another person to shoot and kill Mr. Yablonski." The other person turned out to be a man named Robert Tanner, a Cleveland burglar now a resident of the Ohio penitentiary.

"I seen my wife talking to Robert Tanner several times," Gilly related. "At first she said they were talking about old coins. She told me later Robert Tanner agreed to shoot and kill Mr. Yablonski."

Tanner, he said, "got sent to prison," and Huddleston prevailed on Annette Gilly to bring her husband into the picture. Like the four other accused persons in the case, Gilly was minimizing his own lack of involvement and initiative in the plot against Yablonski. "Mr. Huddleston told me that the union wanted to get rid of Mr. Yablonski. He had messed up the pension funds and other things about the union. Mr. Huddleston asked me did I know anyone who would take care of it . . . shoot Mr. Yablonski."

Gilly said that after much talk, he decided he could find someone. The money, he said, was to total five thousand dollars. He said he was told "the money would be got together from District 19 in small amounts so no one could trace it."

"Who was arranging it?"

"Bill Prater."

"Do you know him?"

"Yes, sitting there." A laconic pointing of the hand indicated defendant Prater. Prater did not flinch but continued resting his left jaw on his hand.

"Mr. Huddleston told me when the money was got together he would let me know the time when Mr. Yablonski would be shot," Gilly went on. He added that the money would be put together by Albert Pass, the secretary-treasurer of District 19, whom he said he never met. Pass was then under indictment in the murders.

Gilly then covered familiar ground—how he hired two other killers, Claude Vealey and James Charles Phillips, the latter dropping out at the last minute to be replaced by Aubran Martin.

In October 1969, Gilly said, he made contact with Prater in Tennessee. Gilly said he asked Huddleston to show him the money for the job. He told of a meeting at Prater's home, where he and Huddleston went to Prater's basement to discuss details, while Annette talked with Prater's wife upstairs. He testified that Mrs. Prater was not informed of what was happening.

Gilly said that when Vealey and Phillips became restless about the money, Gilly "used the name Tony, and told them it was a builder and contractor in Cleveland."

On a return visit to Prater's house in Tennessee, Gilly said, Prater told him, "Albert [Pass] was the boss over the money." He said Prater told him to "stalk Yablonski and shoot and kill him."

Sprague asked whether Prater ever said who wanted Yablonski killed.

"Yes," said Paul Gilly, "Tony Boyle."

Gilly quoted Prater as saying how "fair and great" Boyle was, and how he had turned down offers to be permanent president of the union. "Mr. Prater told me, he said every attempt Mr. Boyle had made to help the pensioners with monthly checks . . . that Mr. Yablonski had blocked them. District Nineteen had made an agreement they would carry this out for Tony Boyle."

Some time after the meeting at Prater's home, Gilly continued, Huddleston came to Cleveland, bringing five thousand dollars with him. He used the bus, said Gilly, so no one could later trace his movements. Gilly depicted himself as the one who was "to get the job done," at Huddleston's direction.

When it came time for Gilly to describe what happened at

the murder scene, he produced a new version of the night of December 31, 1969.

Claude Vealey had confessed that he was there but that his rifle misfired, and that Gilly and Martin took over the shootings. Martin had said he had fallen asleep in the getaway car. Now Paul Gilly testified that he went along with the killings reluctantly and never pulled a trigger.

Telling his story for the first time, Gilly attempted to convey remorse, but he was still painting himself out of the picture.

There were other conflicts in Gilly's story. Annette had said he told her to remember four names if he was arrested—Titler, Owens, Pass, and Prater. Now, Gilly said he told her to remember the names of Boyle, Prater, and Pass. As defense attorney Rothman pointed out, why should Mrs. Gilly have to be reminded to remember Prater's name when she had supposedly met him?

Rothman also ridiculed, by questioning and tone of voice, Gilly's new-found remorse (he had confessed only two days earlier).

"What made you agree to kill Joseph Yablonski?" Rothman asked Gilly.

"A lot of persuasion and folks you listen to—my wife and father-in-law."

Gilly said he was worried that his father, a coal miner, didn't get a pension; but he said his father-in-law, Huddleston, would see that the man got a pension if the murders were committed.

"Silous Huddleston said Joseph Yablonski was responsible for people not getting pensions?" Rothman asked incredulously.

"I believed him," said Gilly.

"Didn't you suggest there might be another way short of murder?"

"No, sir, I did not."

Gilly portrayed himself as having been sucked into the murder plot by his wife Annette and her father Huddleston. Annette, in turn, had depicted her father as the ringleader; while Huddleston had blamed the initiation of the murders on Prater and Albert Pass, as well as Tony Boyle. Clearly, somebody, or everybody, was lying.

Defense attorney Rothman tried to show that Gilly, as a fence for stolen weapons and coins, was merely going to a burglarly at Yablonski's home. Joseph Yablonski was reputed to be a collector of old coins, and so was Gilly—for a price. But on the witness stand, Gilly insisted that he knew the job was murder and that he had discussed it with Prater.

Gilly's story also conflicted with others when he described the carrying out of the murders. He labeled Vealey and Martin as the actual killers and said he tried to talk them out of the job at the last moment, on the Yablonskis' stairway leading to their bedrooms.

"Vealey decided to shoot everybody and not leave any witnesses," Gilly said matter-of-factly in response to questions by Rothman. "Martin backed out on the stairwell. He was talking to Vealey. Vealey came back and got me. I stood at the bottom of the stairwell. The dog was between the two doors. We stayed in the house. Vealey said he wouldn't bark."

"What did he do," asked Rothman, "talk to the dog?"

"Under the circumstances, I wasn't paying much attention to that. He didn't bark and we were willing to trust him."

"Was Vealey a dog lover?"

An objection by Sprague overcame the levity.

Gilly next told of a "whispered discussion" near the bottom of the stairwell as the Yablonskis slept upstairs.

"It was decided then by Vealey that he would shoot Mr. and Mrs. Yablonski and Martin the daughter." said Gilly. Then, he said, Vealey hollered that the gun had jammed.

"I heard the rifle fire one time. In seconds, Vealey hollered that the gun had jammed. I did not hear Mrs. Yablonski scream, or anyone else. I cannot honestly say I never heard them scream. I was scared to death, to tell you the truth about it."

Gilly was shown one of the two murder weapons, but he was adamant.

"I did not shoot anybody or fire one shot," he testified. "I fired this gun in my basement but never fired any other shot. I never left the edge of the stairwell until I went downstairs."

Gilly went on to say he could have stopped the murders in these last minutes but didn't.

"It was another foolish and stupid mistake. I've been sick and sorry ever since, and that's the truth."

But was it? Claude Vealey had told one story. Aubran Martin, protesting his innocence, had told another. Annette Gilly's story conflicted with her husband's.

But Paul Gilly's testimony against Prater was only the start of a parade of contradictions.

A day after Gilly finished came three witnesses—Noah Doss, George Washington Hall, and Corwin Edwin Ross. Like Prater, all were field representatives for the United Mine Workers in District 19. Unlike Prater, they admitted to having received kickbacks of money from members of the "Research and Information Committee." Unlike Prater, they had pleaded guilty to embezzling union money. And unlike Prater, they were still working for the United Mine Workers under the new administration that had replaced Tony Boyle. To defense attorney Rothman, this suggested that cooperation with Sprague and the FBI was the best way for union officials to stay in their jobs and out of a jail cell. To Rothman, the stories the officials told were "fantastic."

Then came the master storyteller of them all—Silous Huddleston. He was in Erie to tell once again his involuted, weird tale of helping to plot the Yablonski murders from his home in Tennessee. Huddleston embellished his bizarre tale even further. Allegedly dying of five diseases simultaneously (the principal one being miner's black lung disease), Silous Huddleston inhaled conspicuously from a portable oxygen device while testifying.

He repeated his story that he planned the murders at the request of Prater and Albert Pass. As president of a retired miners' local in the union, Huddleston was in constant touch with these union officials. But he said he had reasons of his own to want Yablonski killed: Yablonski was going to destroy the union and the pensioners' rights.

Huddleston fingered Prater as the man who channeled $15,000 in union money for the killings. He told the jury that Albert Pass ordered a delay in the killings just before the union election that was won by Tony Boyle. Then, after the election, the word came: Get it done quick.

Incredibly, Huddleston insisted that outsiders wanted Yablonski to defeat Tony Boyle—the same line Boyle himself used. And Huddleston went further: He said the outsiders included the Continental Oil Company. Continental Oil—the parent firm of the nation's second-largest coal company, Consolidation Coal? *They* wanted the union taken over by a rebel who charged that Boyle was too close to the coal operators?

There was good reason for Sprague to put this man on the witness stand. The prosecutor felt that it was important to show the union wanted Yablonski killed even after he lost the election to Boyle.

"I think I can win this case," David Rothman said during a luncheon break before he cross-examined Silous Huddleston. The defense attorney reasoned that the slimy creatures the prosecution had to resort to would be less credible than his client, who had never been arrested. The prosecution's witnesses included an habitual burglar, a convicted rapist, two confessed killers, a larcenist, and several confessed embezzlers.

But Rothman reckoned without the emotional pull of the group of elderly miners, led by "holiness preacher" David Brandenburg. Sprague paraded them into the courtroom. There was Louie Lowe, presenting an abject picture of a miner who had been used all his life, by the industry and now by Sprague. There was his brother Billy Lowe, who signed his name with an X, even when Prater presented checks for him to cash. There was Harvey Huddleston, the miner who had undergone brain surgery for a clot when the union said he was out organizing.

All these men and Brandenburg testified that they had lied previously to grand juries investigating the murders. They had lied by saying they received the union money and spent it on organizing other miners. They said they had been forced to lie and they had kicked back the money. They lied, they said, because of fear. They overpowered the courtroom and the jury with their hopelessness.

Bronce Waldroop, from Clearfield, Tennessee: "I lied because of my hospital card and union benefits. I was afraid of losing them. . . . But then it just hurt me inside. I couldn't rest."

Clifford Marcum, from Speedwell, Tennessee: "Prater told me not to tell anybody I gave the money back. I got scared that something might happen to me or my family. . . . Then God got ahold of me and I couldn't rest till I got it off my chest."

(Rothman: "Did God get ahold of you in any particular place?" The defense attorney apologized after courtroom laughter subsided.)

Harvey Huddleston, of Duff, Tennessee: "I had to come clean. I wanted to get rid of it, get it off my mind."

David Brandenburg, of the Independent Church of God, LaFollette, Tennessee: "I knew Albert Pass had influence with Tony Boyle, and he could order my benefits cut off."

Union field representative Noah Doss summed it up for the conscience-stricken miners who were now changing their stories at the behest of the FBI: "A day of reckoning was coming."

After eight days of testimony, Prosecutor Sprague ended his case—the main portion of it, anyway—on the day before spring. Sprague felt he had proved:

—That William Jackson Prater was the conduit for murder money authorized by Tony Boyle in Washington at the request of Albert Pass.

—That the "Research and Information Committee" never existed, but was set up solely on paper to cover the trail of the money.

—That the union, a powerful force in Appalachia, had put pressure on retired miners to lie about the money that passed through their hands.

To counter the prosecution theory of a union connection with the murders, defense attorney Rothman called Tony Boyle as his lead-off witness. Boyle performed obstinately but futilely. Overwhelmed by Sprague's innuendoes, he left more questions behind him than he answered. In short, Boyle did not help Prater one iota, but he did fuel the prosecution gambit that it was he, Boyle, who was really on trial.

Boyle walked into the courtroom like a man who was still a big-time labor leader entering a convention of delegates await-ing his arrival. Nattily dressed, his hair dyed black, he waved at William Jackson Prater at the defendant's table, shook hands with a startled Tom Henderson (who had prosecuted Boyle in 1972 for illegal political contributions), beamed at Prater's jury, and strode to the witness stand like a man eager to testify. In his coat pocket was a copy of the United Mine Workers' consti-tution.

He was on the stand for more than four hours. The story he told under questioning by Prater's lawyer Rothman was basically his own defense to charges that he had somehow ap-proved a fund to finance Yablonski's murder. He said he first heard about the Research and Information Committee in Sep-tember 1968, at the union convention in Denver. There, he said, Albert Pass suggested putting on retired men as part-time union organizers in District 19, and paying them "gasoline and sand-wich money." A year later, Boyle said, Pass came to him, said the men hadn't been paid, and asked for the money. Boyle was "perturbed," told him the union always paid its bills, and ap-proved the expenditure of $20,000. That was the last he knew of it.

In the afternoon, Sprague began his cross-examination. The brunt of Sprague's attack was on Boyle's contention that he did not look into the Research and Information Committee even after reports began filtering out that it might have been used to finance a murder. Boyle evaded, professed not to remember dates, insisted he never examined checks made out to union districts, worked an eighteen-hour day as union president.

"No, I didn't inquire," he finally said.

"I know you didn't," said Sprague, "and I'm asking you now, you were the president of the United Mine Workers, why didn't you?"

"Because I didn't think it was my——I didn't do it," Boyle suddenly shouted, "and I don't think it was a responsibility of mine."

"You didn't do what?" Sprague shot back.

"Find out who the people were that the newspapers were saying that gave the money back as you say."

"Is that what you meant when you said, 'I didn't do it?'"

"Do what?"

"Mr. Boyle, why didn't you, as the president of the United Mine Workers, simply ask who were the people named on these checks?"

"Well, I didn't do it."

"I know you didn't do it, and is the reason because you knew what that money was used for?"

"Absolutely—I don't know what the money was used for, other than for organizational purposes."

"Then why didn't you make an attempt to find out what it was used for?" Sprague persisted.

"Because the auditors were in there and found the vouchers."

"And then did you decide, I am Tony Boyle, let me talk to Mr. Doss, Mr. Hall, and Mr. Ross and others, and let me ask them, 'What did you do when you got these checks?' Did you do that?"

"No, I didn't do that."

"Why not?"

"I don't know what they would have told me."

"What were you afraid they would have told you?"

Rothman jumped up with an objection, sustained by Judge

Carney, but the tension in the packed courtroom was mounting as Boyle volunteered: "I am not afraid of anything!"

"Nothing, Mr. Boyle?" said Sprague.

Rothman objected again, but before the judge could rule, Boyle retorted: "I fear Almighty God, if that's what you mean."

"No, no," said the judge.

Sprague: "I object to this."

Judge Carney: "We are getting off the track."

Boyle: "I fear Him."

Sprague, seizing an opening, muttered, "I hope you do!"

The cross-examination droned on for more than two hours. Boyle stuck to his story, Prater's name was hardly mentioned, and afterward even Boyle had to agree that he was made to appear a defendant instead of a witness. "From his attitude in his questioning," Boyle said of Sprague, "you'd think that I was on trial instead of someone else."

Rothman also called another witness who damaged the defense. Aubran Martin, the convicted triggerman, repeated his story that he had fallen asleep in the getaway car, unaware that a murder was going on. But in one defiant courtroom confrontation with Sprague, young Martin destroyed his usefulness to Prater.

Cross-examining Martin, Sprague showed that Martin had been subpoenaed for the prosecution but, from his jail cell, had refused.

"I'm already sentenced to die, there's not too much to talk about," Martin explained.

Sprague then waved a letter that Martin had written to the prosecutor.

"Would you like to read it to the jury?"

"Sure."

"I knew you would."

Martin then read: "Sprague: Don't call me to Erie for that trial. I have nothing to say. So if you force me to be present, I will disrupt the courtroom. You had better dig it. P.S.: I used your subpoena to wipe my ass on!"

Martin explained, "I couldn't understand why Mr. Sprague wanted me to testify for him when he didn't believe my story at my trial. He pressed so hard to have me electrocuted in the electric chair."

Sprague then asked Martin: "Did you stop to think we might think you would tell the truth here?"

Martin: I'm telling the truth right now.

Sprague: You are?

Martin: Yes.

Sprague: That's all.

The climax of Prater's defense came when he testified in his own behalf. Confident on the witness stand, he made a flat denial that he had had anything to do with the Yablonski murders. He denied ever discussing the murder plot with Silous Huddleston. And in denying there was a murder fund, Prater followed point by point the story told by Tony Boyle. Prater's face maintained its normally flushed appearance as he unreeled his denials. His stern-faced wife and six of their seven children sat on the front row of the courtroom.

"I never talked to anyone about any such plan," Prater said.

But on cross-examination, Sprague hammered away at a series of meetings Prater held in motels in Kentucky and Tennessee, after the murders. The meetings were with a daughter and granddaughter of Silous Huddleston. Their purpose, according to Sprague, was to transfer $23,000 to the women, for Huddleston's legal defense.

No, said Prater, the meetings were not for that purpose. He said he signed in at the motels under his own name, and his only purpose was to "have a good time." All told, the evidence showed, there were eighteen meetings in 1970 and 1971 with Huddleston's kinfolk. Prater said he may have given the women fifty or a hundred dollars for their own expenses, but it was nothing like twenty-three thousand. Sprague contended that the union raised the money by tapping miners for hundred-dollar contributions every two weeks.

"If you weren't talking with them about money," Sprague asked Prater, "why were you meeting them?"

Prater broke into a wide grin.

"We liked to have a good time," he said. "They liked me to bring some whisky and cigarettes along and have a little party."

"Did you ever go to bed with any of these women?" asked Sprague.

"No, sir, absolutely not."

To attack the prosecution theory of a union-sponsored murder fund, Prater's attorney called one other key witness—Albert Edward Pass, who was awaiting trial as the seventh defendant in the Yablonski murders. Pass had been secretary-treasurer of the union's District 19, a $26,000-a-year job, but he had been in jail almost a year awaiting trial.

Pass was a slight, innocuous-looking man who had been in the union movement for thirty years. He was fifty-two years old, and, at the time he awaited trial, flat broke. His wife was on welfare in Kentucky, and they had an invalid daughter, a victim of cerebral palsy.

As an international executive board member of the union, Pass was a close associate of Tony Boyle.

The story Pass told on behalf of William Prater was basically his own defense: that he first told Boyle about a union organizing job in the fall of 1968, more than a year before the Yablonski murder was allegedly conceived.

Pass denied telling Prater that Yablonski had to be eliminated. "Certainly," Pass said, "there was no advantage to me personally or officially in the death of Joe Yablonski."

Pass denied, too, that the Research and Information Committee was set up to channel murder money. Its purpose, he said, was "to preach the gospel of the union among the non-union coal miners."

Pass was unable, however, to explain adequately why he

waited a full year to write to Boyle asking for $20,000 to pay the preachers of the gospel.

Despite a spirited grilling by Sprague, Pass insisted that the committee was a legitimate enterprise, not a coverup for a murder treasury.

Before the Prater trial went to the jury, Sprague produced one more surprise involving a newly changed story. It came from the president of the union's District 19, William Turnblazer, who was also a lawyer. He admitted having lied to grand juries about his involvement in the Research and Information Committee. Turnblazer now stated that the committee never existed, that it was not set up in the fall of 1968, as Pass had testified.

For the final day of the Prater trial, there were emotional summations by the two attorneys—and another cryptic reference to Tony Boyle. Leading off, Rothman spent two hours telling the jury his client was being railroaded. He said the federal government was out to get Tony Boyle. "He's been on trial ever since the murders three years ago. There's no doubt about it. He's been tried and convicted in the newspapers. And God help us if that is how justice is served in this country."

Sprague, too, discussed Tony Boyle, telling the jury: "This case is not over by a long shot. As I said to you in the beginning, we're starting at the end but we're going back to the beginning."

Sprague said he had no doubt there was no Research and Information Committee. "Why is Tony Boyle lying about that?" he shouted to the jury. "Because there you have the beginning, the person that set this chain of events in motion." Sprague had put Boyle in the defendant's chair.

The jury retired at four-thirty in the afternoon of March 26. Rothman, baggy-eyed and exhausted, left the courthouse with Mrs. Prater and her children. Sprague, superstitious as ever, never left the courthouse, but played chess in a backroom of the D.A.'s office.

The jury came back late—it was almost 11:30 P.M. There was sobbing in the courtroom; it came from Prater's twelve-year-old daughter. As Prater was brought in, he smiled faintly to his family, but his face was ashen pale.

The jury stood up in its box and passed on its written verdict to a clerk. He read it aloud: Guilty on all three counts of murder. Minutes later, the courtroom was deserted, and Prater was back in his cell, sobbing uncontrollably.

His family was preparing to return to LaFollette. Rothman was telling news reporters he would seek a new trial. Sprague was asked for elaboration of his latest reference to Tony Boyle. The prosecutor turned away all questions with a no-comment.

The next morning, Judge Carney announced he was setting a June trial date for Albert Pass. Pass's lawyer moved to seek another change of venue and to get federal charges of conspiracy tried quickly.

And William Jackson Prater, newly convicted on all three counts of murder, sat down in his cell and, in a careful hand, wrote out a confession of his role in the Joseph Yablonski murders.

10

The Marker

ALBERT EDWARD PASS, the man who had run District 19 of the United Mine Workers for more than a decade, was led from the lockup in the rear of the courthouse and up to the second-floor courtroom where his friend William Prater had been convicted three months earlier. The manacles were removed from Pass's wrists, and he was handed a copy of the charges accusing him of the murders of Joseph, Margaret, and Charlotte Yablonski.

Prosecutor Sprague got out of his car, accompanied by two detectives. He was limping on crutches and a foot cast, a token of a recent tennis injury. Asked how the trial might go, Sprague tapped one hand three times on a crutch and smiled. "It will be very interesting to see how a one-legged prosecutor performs."

It was the first Monday in June 1973, and Erie was drenched in sunshine. The air was muggy, and few breezes wafted off the nearby Lake Erie. Flushed by his victory three months earlier in the Prater trial, Sprague hobbled into the courtroom and again read over the *coup de grâce* he held against Albert Pass: the confession by William Prater that had come by ordinary mail to the Philadelphia district attorney's office.

When spectators arrived, they passed through the same metal-detectors that had been set up at Prater's trial. Judge Edward H. Carney was presiding again, and was again imposing tight security precautions.

Pass, a slight, balding man whose face was in a continual
grin, sat at the defendant's table and watched his lawyer, Harold
H. Gondelman, one of Pittsburgh's finest, begin the process of
jury selection. Tall, imperious, with a full head of wavy silver
hair, Gondelman was a criminal lawyer in the classic mode: He
believed in thoroughly prepared speeches, in nitpicking every
chink in the prosecution's armor, in lengthy legal arguments.
Gondelman was also highly paid: He received some $19,000
from Pass, cash in advance—far less than the eventual cost.

The fees stopped, but he was defending Pass, he said, because as a lawyer he couldn't refuse.

It took five days to pick a jury for Pass's trial. Gondelman
fought most of the way along this line of reasoning: The community was already prejudiced against his client because of the
massive publicity in the case. Gondelman had been successful
in having both the Pass and Prater trials taken out of Washington County, but now he argued that one man was responsible
for whipping up community sentiment in Erie against the defendants: Prosecutor Richard Sprague.

After the jury was finally agreed on, Gondelman argued
again, to Judge Carney in his chambers, that it was not a fair
jury—that more than 50 percent of those questioned had a fixed
opinion against Pass. Judge Carney rejected the argument and
the trial began, after a weekend recess.

Sprague led off with a big punch—his opening statement,
which he delivered, as usual, without notes. The prosecutor was
bothered by his injured right ankle, and he apologized to the
jurors for sitting on the edge of the prosecution table. Although
Pass was the only defendant in the case then facing trial,
Sprague told the jurors that this wasn't the end of the line:

"You'll hear evidence which has led the authorities not just
to get the ones who pulled the trigger, as all too often happens,
and that's where cases end, but you'll hear how step by step this
case is going from what I say is the end, the assassination, back
to the beginning, where as sure as you are sitting there, that's
where this case is going to end up, back at the beginning. . . .

"This case is not complicated, members of the jury. We start at the end, the assassination of a man striving to clean up a union, and you will hear how the steps that Jock Yablonski took survived his death, for you will hear how the steps that he initiated after he lost that election, to reverse that election, succeeded.

"They couldn't kill the concept of cleaning up that union. . . . They tried to preserve Boyle's hold within the union but they couldn't succeed even with that death.

"What I say to you, members of the jury, listen intently to this case because it doesn't stop here, and it's not going to. You have the task of deciding the guilt or innocence of this defendant. . . . He's not the arranger, he's one of those, and we don't stop, and don't you throw a monkey wrench into it as you hear this case."

Defense attorney Gondelman was tempted to object to this appeal to the jury—no one but Pass was then awaiting trial. But he let the "monkey wrench" remark slide by rather than reinforce Sprague's statement.

As he rose to make his opening statement, Gondelman presented a striking contrast with the prosecutor. Sprague was short and hobbled by a cast; Gondelman stood ramrod straight and walked gracefully. Sprague spoke extemporaneously; Gondelman used a formal lectern and notes. Sprague was ashen pale; Gondelman was tanned from the golf course. And while Sprague declaimed in rich, sonorous cadences every point he wished to emphasize, the defense lawyer spoke in informal but strident sentences in a voice that, when angered, rose to a high pitch. Gondelman pleaded for the jurors to keep an open mind, indicated he would rely chiefly on character testimony for his principal defense, and described the main prosecution witnesses as murderers who were not to be believed. "You must decide in your mind, 'Am I going to believe what's coming out of the mouth of that murderer?' "

Well before the Pass trial started, Sprague marshaled his forces at the Holiday Inn a few miles from the Erie courthouse.

A mixed crew took over forty rooms—FBI agents, state police, the elderly miners from Tennessee and Kentucky, legal assistants, secretaries, former officials of the union in Washington. At other motels, under state police guard, were Annette Gilly, her husband Paul, and Silous Huddleston; in nearby jails were Claude Vealey and James Charles Phillips. In all, nearly 150 witnesses were ready to testify against Albert Pass, but only one of them was the subject of Sprague's most important prep session in the Yablonski case—William Jackson Prater.

Federal marshals brought Prater to Sprague's suite of rooms at the Holiday Inn. He walked in like a salesman—shoes shined, fresh white shirt and tie under his neat jacket, confident, not quite smiling but not downcast, either. Sprague wasn't in the suite when Prater arrived at 10:00 P.M., and at first he seemed ill at ease, but then he warmed up to the FBI agents and Sprague's assistants. His face was flushed and his curly gray hair was neatly combed, and he stretched out his hands to his fellow southerner, FBI agent Henry Quinn, and told him: "I want to thank you for what you've done for my wife. She's told me you've been very nice to her. You were polite at all times and you stopped in to see how she's doing. I appreciate that. You know, one of my sons told me after my trial, 'Dad, if I'd been on that jury, I would have had to convict you.' "

Sprague came in on his crutches. The men were going to talk in a bedroom, where Sprague wanted to rest his injured ankle. Prater assisted him, looking for all the world like a man who wanted to be part of the team.

Prater sat at the foot of Sprague's bed, telling the prosecutor: "Now that my feather has fallen, I might as well come clean." He appeared to have everything well thought out. As soon as Sprague asked one question—"Tell me how you got involved in this"—Prater launched into a twenty-minute explanation about his loyalty to the union, what the union had done for him.

Sprague sized up the man before him, trying to get a feel for what he would be like on the witness stand at Albert Pass's trial. Prater tried earnestly to remember details, and he did—precise intersections in LaFollette, Tennessee, where he had spoken to Albert Pass about Jock Yablonski, exact places where he had met Silous Huddleston.

Why was he talking now? "I didn't want my family to think that there had been a government conspiracy to convict me," he said. "I didn't want them to think the charges were trumped up."

Was he remorseful? "I was destroyed when I heard that those women were killed," he said.

Why had he lied at his own trial? He said he had gotten together with Pass many times in prison, they had gone over their stories, they would stick by each other, and they never dreamed they could be convicted. "Then, suddenly, I saw it was useless," said Prater. "I've gone far enough for Albert Pass."

Sprague listened for nearly an hour, then had some of the old miners brought into the suite. The prosecutor wanted to solidify whatever testimony the old men might give by showing them that the leader of the "Prater cell," as Sprague called it, was now cooperating. In came Harvey Huddleston, Billy Lowe, Louis Lowe, Clifford Marcum, three or four others.

"I know you want an opportunity to speak with them," Sprague told Prater. Prater nodded.

The men were fifteen to twenty years older than Prater, but they looked up to him; he was their field representative in the union, and they had been through a lot together. After shaking hands with each of them and embracing two or three, Prater made a little speech.

"I want to thank y'all very much," he said. "You've done more for me over the past few years than any man can expect from a friend. You lied for me before the grand juries. You stood by me, and now have seen the light. I must do what is right for my family and for myself. But I wanted you to know that Mr. Sprague was kind enough to give me an opportunity to tell y'all personally, I will never forget you for what you've done for me all these years, by lying for me all these years."

The old miners all nodded. William Prater was taken out by the marshals, and observers were touched—and chilled.

Late on the afternoon of June 13, 1973, William Jackson Prater was led into Erie's Courtroom Number One to testify against Albert Pass. The weather was warm—nearly seventy degrees—and the chunky, well-scrubbed Prater was perspiring; but his mind was clear and his determination was firm: to do everything Prosecutor Sprague wanted him to do.

First, Prater entered a guilty plea—less than three months after pleading not guilty in the same courtroom. As soon as he took the witness stand, Prater was asked by Sprague why he had made his confession.

"I met with my family here in the Erie County jail," said Prater, "and discussed the case with them, and I seen they were very upset about the outcome of the case. I would have liked to have told them at that time the circumstances that I wanted to make the confession, but I didn't think it was the proper place and time."

Afterward, Prater's attorney had come to see him in jail in Pittsburgh.

"He outlined that I could appeal and everything and after he got through talking to me about that, I told him I didn't want to go in court anymore for any reason other than just to straighten out the things that have been done, and made an oral statement to him. A lot of the things I told him were lies, and I answered some of his questions orally, and he told me, advised me rather, to take my time and write out a statement to the best of my ability as to the facts that were correct, which I did."

Sprague summoned William Curtis of the FBI to read part of the written statement made by Prater. After admitting his role in the murders, Prater said Pass asked him to find someone to kill Yablonski in the summer of 1969.

"Pass told me that something had to be done about Yablonski. Pass said that he wanted Yablonski knocked off or done away with. Pass said that Yablonski knew too much about the union. Albert Pass told me that if Tony Boyle died, Yablonski was just a heartbeat away from being president of the union. Pass wanted to know if I knew anyone who would do the job.

"I believe that Albert Pass contacted me to help in this murder based on my loyalty to the union and due to the fact that in the past when asked to do something, I would do it."

Prater said the murder fund started at $5000, then went to $15,000, and that he recruited Silous Huddleston. He said Pass, at a meeting with Huddleston, gave Huddleston a picture from the UMW *Journal,* with an arrow pointing to Yablonski.

"Albert told us that he preferred that Yablonski be killed in Washington, D.C. Later Albert said he didn't care where it was done."

There was little mention of Tony Boyle in Prater's statement, but at one point he said: "Albert Pass volunteered that Tony Boyle didn't know anything about the murder plan. Pass also made a similar statement sometime after the murder. I thought that this was a strange statement since I had not asked Pass anything about Boyle. In fact, I did not ask Pass any questions at all concerning why the murder plan was back on. Albert Pass is the kind of man you don't question. If he wants you to know something, he will tell you."

After his statement was read, Prater was taken to the federal courthouse across the street where he pleaded guilty to one count of conspiracy. He received a life term in a federal prison for his cooperation. He had been told life is better in federal prisons, and he wanted to spare his family any more horror. In fifteen years, he could become eligible for parole—at the age of sixty-nine.

His tall, proud wife Maxine stood in the federal courtroom and there were no tears in her eyes. Afterward she told reporters: "I told him if I had been on his jury, I would have come up with the same verdict. Some people won't believe this, but there's a lot of good in Bill."

Then it was back to the trial of Albert Pass, where Prater sat calmly on the witness stand and elaborated on his confession.

Q. Did you take part in the arrangements for the killing of Jock Yablonski?

A. Yes, I did.

Q. And did someone contact you and ask you to make those arrangements?

A. Yes, they did.

Q. Who contacted you and asked you to make the arrangements?

A. Albert Pass.

Pass glared at Prater, knowing full well what was coming next. But Prater was unshaken, even relaxed now that it was all coming out.

Q. Do you see Albert Pass in this courtroom?

A. Yes, I do.

Q. Point him out to the jury.

A. That's him right over there at the desk. . . .

Q. Did you and this defendant get together before your own trial with regard to your testimony?

A. Yes, we did.

Q. Tell the jury what occurred.

A. How far back should I go, sir?

Q. Let me ask you this: Even before your own trial, did you go before a number of federal grand juries and testify under oath?

A. Yes, I did.

Q. Approximately five different times?

A. I testified before the federal grand jury, Ohio, Mr. Sprague, on different occasions. I also testified on one occasion before the federal grand jury at London, Kentucky.

Q. And on those times that you testified before the federal grand jury, did you lie before the federal grand jury under oath and say how innocent you were and all that sort of stuff?

A. Yes, I did.

Q. Now my question to you is: Before you went before those

*grand juries, as well as your own trial, did you discuss with this
defendant, Albert Pass, what you would testify to?*

A. Yes, I did.

Q. Tell the jury what happened.

A. Over the long period of time after the murder took place,
in the last of 1969, we discussed it on many different occasions,
about what we would say if anything happened, any of us got
picked up, and it covers a wide range, this research and information, also the actual contacts made about the arrangements for
the murder and some of the agreements that we made between
each other, was I would testify that I had never taken Silous
Huddleston or met with him in regard to the Yablonski case.

*Q. Did you agree with this defendant to testify that you took
no part in any arrangement for the murder?*

A. Yes, I did.

Q. Was that true or false?

A. That was a false statement that I was to testify to.

Prater was asked to relate when Pass first discussed killing
Yablonski. He said Albert Pass first approached him in the
middle of 1969, shortly after Yablonski had announced his candidacy for the union presidency. "He was discussing the fact
that Joe Yablonski had announced his candidacy for the president of the United Mine Workers and making some derogatory
statements in regard to Mr. Yablonski," said Prater. "He said
something needed to be done about Joe Yablonski, and in kind
of an urgent tone of voice, and I thought he meant maybe a
possible scare, and I told him I didn't know anyone that might
be interested or know anything about that. And then he went
on to indicate to me that he wasn't interested in a scare campaign, that the man had to be done away with altogether, completely."

To reinforce Prater's effect on the jury, Sprague repeated
in a loud voice: "What did this defendant Albert Pass say he
wanted done with Joe Yablonski?"

"He said Joe Yablonski needed to be knocked off."

Albert Pass sat in the witness chair and never squirmed as
Prater unraveled the story of how he recruited Silous Huddleston to find the killers, how Huddleston kept checking back on
the progress of the murder contract during the summer of 1969.
Pass listened intently as Prater told of meetings among the three
of them—meetings always held near the driveway of Pass's
home in Middlesboro, Kentucky.

On one occasion, said Prater, the three of them went inside
Pass's home, and Pass gave a picture to Huddleston.

"There was more than one person in the picture," said
Prater, "but I remember seeing a check mark to Joe Yablonski
as being the proper person."

"Who put that mark on the picture?"

"I didn't see who put the mark on the picture, but it was
on there when Albert Pass handed it to Silous Huddleston. I
did see the mark."

The murder plans went forward and Huddleston recruited
his son-in-law Paul Gilly, and soon Annette Gilly was in on the
plans, too, said Prater. In late November 1969, he said, Pass met
with Huddleston at the Knoxville airport and asked him to tell
his people "to hold up on the execution, the murder, and Silous
told him he was sure he could."

Q. Did Pass say why he wanted the plan held up?

A. Yes, he did.

Q. What did he say?

A. He said he wanted it held up because the election was
drawing too near, that if anything happened to Joe Yablonski
that the general public would have the idea he was killed to prevent him from being elected president of the International Union
of Mine Workers, and it had been determined that he would
not win the presidency of the United Mine Workers of America.
Therefore, there was no use killing him before the election.

Q. After that, what then occurred?

A. It was some days after the election. Albert Pass told me
that he'd received the green light or the go-ahead notice to go
ahead with this plan.

Q. Stop right there. Pass said he received the green light?

A. He used this expression, "I received the green light to proceed," or "I received the go-ahead to proceed." It was either one of the phrases, to the best of my recollection.

Q. What did he then tell you to do?

A. He told me to contact Silous Huddleston at the earliest possible minute and tell him the ante would be raised to fifteen thousand dollars if the job was done by the first of the year. And I went straight to Silous's home and told him.

Prater said Pass later turned over another five thousand dollars, and that Paul Gilly was instructed to hold up on the Yablonski murder until the first of the new year. Prater said he heard the news of the Yablonski murder on television on January 5, 1970, that he called Pass, who said, "Some of the members have called in. I'm going to try to confirm it." Meanwhile, he said, Huddleston came to his house.

"And he came over and came to my back door and I had removed the envelope from the cabinet, the filing cabinet I had, and I had the money at that time in a big brown envelope with 'United Mine Workers of America, District Nineteen,' in the upper lefthand corner on it, and I noticed that, and I dumped the money in a brown paper sack out of that envelope, and I destroyed the envelope. And when Silous came to the door I met him and handed him the money in the paper sack, and we had very few words, just kind of greeted, and he left."

"That was the final nine thousand dollars for the murder?"

"Yes, this was what I had in my possession."

Sprague paused and surveyed the jury.

He seldom paused, usually jumping on a witness's last sentence, in order to build a coherent story. Now he paused until he was convinced that the jury was giving its fullest attention, then went on:

"Mr. Prater, why did you participate in making arrangements to kill Joe Yablonski?"

"The reason I participated in the thing, Mr. Sprague, is a long story. I'll make it as brief as I can. Of course, my grandfather and father were coal miners. My father was very active in the United Mine Workers during his lifetime. I went to work in the coal mines in 1937. We didn't have any union then. In 1942 I joined the United Mine Workers and conditions were much better, and I was active from the first day I joined the union. I held office, president of the local union and committee work, and I worked in the coal mines near to twenty years. And I been with the United Mine Workers now something like thirty-four years. I was extremely loyal to the union, and when this was mentioned, when Albert said that this was a very important thing, I thought from his past experience it was something necessary to protect the union. And if I thought I was protecting the union, I went along with it. And after I started I didn't want to get out of it."

A hush came over the courtroom as the red-faced, neat-looking man described why he had followed orders. It was now June of 1973, and though the jury was sequestered from day to day, it was deciding a man's fate in a world in which the national government was being rocked by the most corrupt scandal the nation had ever faced.

William Jackson Prater looked relieved. The sun was still shining, it was late afternoon in Erie, Pennsylvania, and William Prater was telling how he dutifully followed orders that resulted in the deaths of a man and two women. Once again, Sprague let it all sink in, then had one more question. The prosecutor spoke in measured words, and gathered his strength to stand on his injured ankle, going toward Albert Pass as he framed the question:

"Now Mr. Prater, I want you to look at this defendant, Albert Pass, the man you've known from back in the forties. Is there any doubt in your mind that he is the man that contacted you to make the arrangements and put the money through your hands to kill Jock Yablonski?"

Kenneth and Joseph Yablonski, Jr., swung their eyes toward the steely face of Albert Pass, and Prater replied, "None whatsoever, sir."

Defense attorney Gondelman's cross-examination of Prater was, not surprisingly, brief. In Gondelman's mind, there was no point in challenging Prater on the details of his confession as to what happened in 1969. He knew that Sprague could corroborate Prater on every point, with such witnesses as Huddleston, Paul Gilly, Annette Gilly. Instead, Gondelman focused on Prater's reasons for turning state's witness—a federal prison, eventual freedom. But Prater wouldn't be shaken.

"As you sit in this witness chair under oath in this courtroom today, is it your understanding today you are going to be sent to a federal penitentiary if [officials] can make those arrangements for you?" Gondelman asked.

"It was made clear to me in federal court, I think," said Prater, "that I received the life sentence in the federal court, but it would be left up to some board to assign me to a prison on the recommendation of the board. I don't know what kind of act or how the board acts, but they did indicate they would get me to serve my, any time, in the federal penitentiary."

Q. And did that lead you to believe that if those three sentences were to run concurrently, you would have some chance of getting out of jail?

A. I really don't know. I didn't discuss the possibility of getting out of jail.

Q. You were in the Allegheny County jail after the trial here?

A. I been in Allegheny since the trial, yes, sir.

Q. Did you tell anyone, any of the inmates at the Allegheny County jail, that you would lie on Jesus Christ and on Albert Pass and on anybody else because if you did, it would be the only way you had any hopes of ever seeing your family again?

A. No, sir, I never did.

Q. Never made that statement to anybody?

A. No, sir, I never did. . . .

Q. And would you lie to protect yourself?

A. I did that.

Q. And you would now, would you not?

A. No, sir, I would not.

Q. You will not lie today under oath?

A. No, sir, I will not lie today under oath, under no circumstances.

Q. This is to protect your family?

A. I realize my loyalty is to protect any people all the time, and my first loyalty is to protect my family from here on out.

Q. From here on out?

A. That's when I realized, when my trial was over, when I talked to my family at the Erie County Jail. . . .

Q. And you, sir, deny that after you were convicted you told anyone you would lie to get out of jail so that some day you might see your wife and family?

A. Never made no such statement as that to any person at any time.

Prater's testimony was the heart of the prosecution's case against Albert Pass. Prater was so effective and so strong a witness that Sprague felt he could speed things up.

Defense attorney Gondelman was moving quickly, too. He made stipulations that saved time. He dismissed witnesses with perfunctory cross-examinations. He was confident that the jury would not believe the words coming out of what he described as "the mouths of three murderers." Gondelman had high hopes for an acquittal, but failing that, he was confident of building a good record for an appeal.

Sprague moved swiftly with his remaining witnesses. Huddleston once again spun out his tale of accepting the payoff money and arranging for Gilly, Vealey, and Martin to do the deed. Several union representatives confirmed Prater's story of a kickback of money to Albert Pass and of their own previous lies to grand juries. Union comptroller Howard Channell was back on the stand to tell how Boyle authorized the payment of two checks totaling $20,000 to District 19. Gondelman pointed out it was all in the union records, and that there had been no attempt to destroy the records. Noah Doss, Chester Philpot, Corwin Ross, and George Washington Hall told how Albert

Pass forced them to cover up the kickback of the money. Gondelman waved their stories aside with the frequently reiterated observation that it was all in the normal course of union business, with records maintained for all the world to see.

Gondelman was building up for his principal defense—an attack on the credibility of the witnesses, and a defense of Albert Pass's reputation.

The prosecution case was over in four days. Prater's trial had lasted three weeks, but this time Sprague cut corners and was eager to get Pass's fate before the jury. Sprague anticipated Gondelman's key strategy. Albert Pass, a witness for William Prater at his trial, was not going to take the witness stand this time. Neither would Tony Boyle come to Erie again to testify, as he had for Prater. Gondelman was going to risk all on the good name of Albert Pass, exercising his constitutional right not to testify against himself.

Both sides had a difficult task. Since Pass was not directly involved in the actual killings, and since Boyle had won the election of December 9, 1969, Sprague had to show motivation for Pass to want Yablonski killed. For this purpose, he used a number of witnesses, the most effective of whom was Yablonski's son Chip.

Q. Following the election, did your father publicly state his intention to fight within the union?

A. Yes.

Q. And following that, did he then take steps to have the election voided by the federal courts?

A. Yes, he did.

Q. Following your father's death, did the courts subsequently void that election?

A. Yes.

To counter that, Gondelman attempted to insinuate motivation to gain control of the union on Chip Yablonski's part —without creating sympathy for the son of the murdered Yablonski.

Q. Did you ever see a newspaper article, . . . in which you were quoted by the newspaper saying in light of your father's defeat by eighty-thousand to forty-six thousand it made it most difficult to overturn the election?

A. No, I don't recall every seeing such as that. . . .

Q. And during that campaign between Arnold Miller and Tony Boyle, is it not true that the death of your father, mother, and sister were used in the United Mine Workers Journal against Tony Boyle's candidacy?

A. I can recall certain campaign materials in the *Journal* containing references to the murders.

Q. As a result of that election Arnold Miller became the president?

A. Yes.

Q. And you became general counsel?

A. Yes.

Q. And the director of the Washington Bank owned by the UMW?

A. I am a director of the National Bank of Washington.

Harold Gondelman's defense case for Albert Pass went swiftly. Gondelman did not put the defendant on the witness stand; perhaps the defense lawyer remembered the harsh cross-examination of Pass three months earlier when his client attempted to testify on behalf of Prater. Or perhaps he relied on the jury's inherent fairness under American law, which holds that the burden of proof of guilt never shifts from the prosecution; in other words, a defendant does not have to prove his innocence. But in practical fact, it is an axiom of courtrooms that the more serious a case, the more risky it is for a defendant not to get on the witness stand.

At any rate, Gondelman took that risk, and Albert Pass watched a procession of character witnesses from Kentucky testify to his good name and reputation. Sprague let most of them go by without cross-examination; another axiom of courtroom strategy is that you do not challenge witnesses simply for challenge's sake. So the character witnesses were allowed to testify to Albert Pass's good name. There came a doctor, a school superintendent, a lawyer, all of whom said they knew Albert and, yes, he was a good man. Nonetheless, Sprague could not resist a few jabs when the public defender of Harlan County, Kentucky, James C. Brock, said on the stand that Albert Pass's reputation was "very good."

"Is he a close friend to you?" asked Sprague.

A. No.

Q. Not a close friend to you?

A. Not a close friend, I don't know him that well.

Q. You don't know him that well?

A. No, sir.

Q. What made you go around asking people what his reputation was?

A. I didn't go around asking people what his reputation was.

Q. That's all.

Gondelman tried to save this witness's testimony by asking Brock whether he had discussed Pass's reputation. "Yes, sir," said Brock. But Sprague, unwilling to yield, shot back:

Q. Did you talk with Tony Boyle about Albert Pass?

A. I don't know Tony Boyle.

Q. Did you ever meet with him?

A. Never saw him in my life.

Q. That's all.

Out of such cameos is a prosecution case built or lost, and Sprague was again forceful on Gondelman's second strategy—to impute self-serving motives to prosecution witnesses. In order to show that Prater had lied, Gondelman summoned two former inmate acquaintances of Prater, who testified that Prater had told them he'd lie against Albert Pass or anyone else to get out of jail. Prater was recalled by Sprague and denied the allegation. To reinforce Prater's testimony, Sprague called in the two scruffy-looking ex-convicts and let the jury contrast them with the well-scrubbed, sincere-looking Prater.

As a final tactic, Gondelman wanted Judge Carney to call

Paul Gilly as a court witness. That would enable Gondelman to cross-examine Gilly on the defense's terms. Sprague, in his opening statement to the jury, had said he would call Gilly, but never did. Pointing out that omission, Gondelman argued, out of hearing of the jury, that for the defense to summon Gilly would be to open him up to cross-examination by the prosecutor. That would put in all kinds of testimony damaging to the defense.

Gondelman lost this legal chess game. The judge refused to call Gilly and said the defense had that option. Gondelman's point in calling Gilly was to have him testify that other murderers—Vealey, Huddleston, Annette Gilly—were offered deals by which they would be out of jail when the case was over. Again, motivation of the accusers was important to the defense. But after a brief meeting with Gilly outside the courtroom, Gondelman learned that Gilly would be able to provide only rumors about the other murderers. So rather than place a damaging witness on the stand, Gondelman gave up on Gilly and closed his defense. Both sides were now ready to unload their closing speeches to the jury.

A midafternoon breeze swept over downtown Erie and sunshine poured into Courtroom Number One as Harold Gondelman got up to make his last pitch for Albert Pass. The tall defense attorney adjusted a lectern, piled his notes high on it, and was off in a rush—too much of a rush, since Pass was not even back in the courtroom.

"Do you want to wait for your client?" Sprague interjected as Gondelman began his torrent of words to the jury. Sheepishly the defense attorney paused, looked around, then mumbled an apology. Albert Pass was led in, and Gondelman began again.

He spoke for thirty-five minutes, in an outraged nasal tone, imploring the seven men and five women of the jury to remember that the defendant is always "clothed with the armor of the presumption of innocence until that armor is stripped from him beyond a reasonable doubt by the evidence of the Commonwealth of Pennsylvania.

"And he doesn't have to, and under the Constitution he has the right not to take the stand in this courtroom but to say to you, as I say to you, has the Commonwealth proved its case?

"Credibility," said Gondelman, his voice rising in scorn, "That's what this case is all about. Can you believe a man who gets on that witness stand? . . .

"I say to you that the facts in this case are so completely false from these witnesses that you cannot possibly rely on them in your deliberations."

He pointed out that Claude Vealey had confessed two years earlier, and had not yet been sentenced. The same with Huddleston and the rest—the sentence was a "sword of Damocles" for their continued cooperation with the prosecution.

"I say to you," he went on, "in this courtroom you can't buy the testimony of one Commonwealth witness because they are liars and perjurers and under the control of the government and of the Commonwealth of Pennsylvania and even the federal government in Washington, D.C."

It was late in the day when Sprague hobbled to the front of the defense table—as always, without notes—and began his summation to the jury. He invoked the mood of the summer afternoon and contrasted it with the horror of the New Year's Eve murders of three years earlier. He spoke for forty-five minutes, and used props, such as the murder rifle and gun, and harsh, cold winter words:

"What is this case about? You know as we sit here today, sit in a lighted courtroom area, it is difficult to go back, time has a way of erasing things. . . . Christmas season, 1969, there lurking literally upon their home on those hills—you saw the picture—sat killers. . . . There on those hills sat gunmen armed with this weapon, and we go back and think of that time three years ago and now this courtroom becomes sterile in a sense. But just think, right here in my hand, I am offering a weapon that snuffed somebody's life out, that shot somebody, just think, right here in front of you. And again how sterile it appears. . . . What this case is about, members of this jury, has nothing to do with the members of the Pass family who sit here. All this case has to do with is who hired these people, who was it that brought those assassins that were lurking in the hills, hired to murder, and murder they did."

The prosecutor turned toward Albert Pass, sitting halfway across the room. "I suggest to you that one of the people is this defendant, is Pass sitting right there." Sprague paused again, changed the subject, denounced the killers, then examined the matter of the murder money.

"Foolproof, foolproof," he exclaimed, his deep Philadelphia accent echoing to the rear of the high courtroom. "Who would think that the federal authorities—and I take my hat off to them—who would think that with the millions of dollars that were spent in that union, with one hundred and some thousand dollars that in 1969 went into District 19 . . . who would think that the authorities with all that was involved, the millions of dollars in checks, could narrow it down, narrow it down to one area. . . .

"You know, you may say to yourselves, 'Gee, did he have such a hold over them? So what if they lose their jobs?' Did you see some of these people? You ask yourselves, those people that had worked for thirty or forty years in the mines, here they all of a sudden have no other means of income, no livelihood, what happens to them? Do you think they can just get themselves another job? . . . But who was it that got them to lie? The defendant that sits there."

Paul Gilly's jury had been told he was the "captain of the enterprise." Aubran Martin had been described as "the baby-faced killer." Prater had been "the conduit." Now, for Albert Pass, Sprague coined a new epithet:

"Who is it that literally marked Jock Yablonski for death? Who is it that drew on that diagram the marking for the killers to be able to identify those three people, or showed in that picture which one was Jock Yablonski?

"The marker. The person who marked them for extinction,

assassination, sits right here. You have a duty to do. Don't flinch from it."

On the morning of the eighth day of his trial, Albert Pass watched his jury file out slowly to deliberate. He himself was then led out to repose in a jail cell next door. He said good-by to his wife and son, the ever-present smile still on his face.

The morning dragged into afternoon and still the jury wasn't back. Sprague played chess in a back room of the D.A.'s office. He played his teenage son and lost, beat one reporter at the board, let the time go by, in a serene mood, drank his chocolate malted. Gondelman went out for lunch, expressing confidence that the jury would rule in his client's favor.

At four-thirty, after nearly seven hours of deliberation, the jury sent out word: It had reached a verdict. Albert Pass came in, smiled at his wife and children, gave them a "Keep your chin up" gesture with his fist. The jurors filed into the courtroom, none of them looking at the defendant. No one in the courtroom —even Pass—seemed surprised when the verdict was read: Guilty on all three counts of murder in the first degree. Albert Pass was escorted out of the courtroom, and he was no longer smiling.

In front of the courthouse as the afternoon played itself out, Prosecutor Richard Sprague favored his injured leg, and before getting into his car to prepare for his return to Philadelphia, he made a statement to reporters. Albert Pass, the seventh of the defendants in the Yablonski murder case, was now convicted, and for the first time in three years no one was under indictment for the Yablonski killings.

"There will be at least one more arrest in this case," said Sprague. "The green light for the Yablonski murder was given in Washington, and we will take the case back to the beginning."

And what about Tony Boyle? Sprague was asked.

"What *about* Tony Boyle?" Sprague replied.

11

"Tony Boyle's Doin' Fine"

ALBERT PASS WAS always a good union man. Albert Pass was always tough. He had to be, to survive the quarreling and brawling and even killing that went on among the miners of Tennessee, Kentucky, and Alabama. It was dangerous underground and it was dangerous on the surface, where the union fought the nonunion coal companies, a rival labor union (whose headquarters were once dynamited), and sometimes the strike-breaking sheriffs. The miners fought so hard in one part of Kentucky that they had a special name for the county—Bloody Harlan. And Albert Pass was so tough that, in union matters, he could sometimes out-tough Tony Boyle.

There was the morning of June 23, 1969. Scene: the United Mine Workers international executive board room at the union's headquarters not far from the White House. Time: shortly after 11:00 A.M. On hand: more than fifty men, members of the international executive board, like Albert Pass, and district presidents, like William Turnblazer from District 19. Among the IEB members also was the newly announced candidate for international president, Jock Yablonski, and presiding was Tony Boyle.

John L. Lewis had died twelve days earlier, and the union leadership wore their mourning faces. Jock Yablonski was expecting Tony Boyle to oust him that day from the IEB. "But we fooled him," Boyle said later. Jock remained on the IEB, but Albert Pass got up and spoke on behalf of his leader, taking, as Boyle liked to observe of the District 19 secretary-treasurer, "quite a lead."

No one resented the candidacy of Jock Yablonski more than Pass. He attacked the opposition of the "outsiders" who were behind Yablonski. He spoke to the IEB "as an officer and member of the United Mine Workers." As Tony Boyle listened gratefully, Albert Pass turned to his presiding officer and declared:

"We have got a great union and we are going to keep our union. President Boyle, we are not going to leave you and the other officers sitting out in that field, and these damned fellows behind the bushes shooting at you, by yourself. By God, we will run them out from behind those bushes. We are going to back you."

Such kudos never annoyed Boyle. He regarded them as his due, as president of the union of more than 200,000 men. In his dreamier moments he gazed at the enormous picture of the great John L. on the fourth floor of union headquarters, or he stopped and glanced at the huge black bust of John L., made entirely of coal, at the main staircase, and imagined himself, one day, enshrined in the union's pantheon.

The first step toward that enshrinement came at the June 23 meeting of the IEB: The board voted to fill a vacancy on the three-member Welfare and Retirement Fund. The nominee would replace the union trustee who had died, President-emeritus Lewis. The IEB selected W. A. Boyle to fill Lewis's shoes on the Fund. It was an important decision, because it gave Boyle the leverage he needed to increase the pensions of retired miners—and that, he hoped, would insure his reelection in 1969.

Yablonski arrived at the meeting at 10:45 A.M. He was prepared to mount a legal challenge to any attempt to oust him from the IEB. He had asked Boyle for permission to bring a lawyer to the meeting. That was never done, Boyle said, and Yablonski came alone. Yablonski had also sent a letter to Boyle before the meeting; Boyle later claimed he did not receive the letter until after the meeting. It asked that Yablonski be repre-

sented by counsel when the matter of his status on the board
came up. "This is not a court of law, there will be no lawyers,"
Boyle later said he told Yablonski.

That Boyle was angered by Yablonski's candidacy, announced three weeks earlier, there was no doubt. Some observers remember Boyle's being particularly rankled by Ralph Nader's role in Yablonski's kickoff press conference. They said
Boyle referred to Nader as "that camel rider from Lebanon."
He resented Nader's "outsider" status and he objected to Nader's critical letter to John L. Lewis, just before Lewis's death,
in which Nader blasted the leadership of Tony Boyle. Boyle
doesn't specifically remember referring to Nader as "that camel
rider" at the June 23 meeting, but he doesn't deny saying it,
either. In Boyle's own words, in August 1969: "I don't recall.
I could use lots of statements about Mr. Nader, because Mr.
Nader started off in the first instance making a lot of statements
about the president of the international union. . . . If I didn't
say it then, I will say it now."

Boyle could be tough. He once told Joseph Rauh, Yablonski's attorney: "Now listen, don't you question my integrity,
because I will get up and walk out of this place before I will
have you impugn my integrity. I told you the facts, and I told
you the truth. And if you don't want to accept them, I am not
going to sit here and be insulted by Joe Rauh. I don't have to
and I won't. . . . You have got a reputation of insulting people,
and you are not going to insult me."

Tony Boyle could be tough, but he could be insouciant and
cloying, too. At the same legal meeting where he warned Rauh
not to insult his integrity, Boyle tried to feign surprise at Yablonski's announcement of candidacy. Boyle maintained that all
he was interested in was having Yablonski doing his job as
union lobbyist. Trying to conceal the rage and panic Yablonski's
candidacy caused the union leadership, Boyle told this story of
how he got the word of Yablonski's announcement:

"I arrived at the office between eight-fifteen and eight-thirty
on the morning of the twenty-ninth. Around nine o'clock, or

shortly after nine o'clock, several calls came in with respect to the Mine Workers' position on legislation. Which prompted me, as I looked at the clock at nine o'clock on the morning of the twenty-ninth, to call Mr. Yablonski's office. And I was apprised by his secretary that he hadn't shown up and was not there.

"I said, 'Well, maybe he went directly to the Hill, because this legislation is in trouble. Maybe he is over on the Hill.'

"I tried to locate him, because there were several people that I wanted to contact on the Hill, in regard to what the Mine Workers will or will not do on this legislation.

"She was unable to locate Mr. Yablonski. . . .

"The reason Mr. Yablonski was not over on the Hill was because when the teletype came in, the first knowledge I had of it, it said on the teletype that a private press conference was held at the Mayflower Hotel announcing his candidacy for the office of president of the United Mine Workers of America. . . .

"He should have been over on the Hill promoting the safety legislation for the United Mine Workers of America.

"As far as making his announcement of his candidacy was concerned, it could have waited to a more opportune time when our bills weren't in trouble, he could have waited until a weekend if he wanted to."

How did William Anthony Boyle get to be president of the United Mine Workers of America? It was a combination of political skill, good health (he was past sixty when he assumed the presidency), and luck. The skill came in doing John L. Lewis's bidding as troubleshooter, always staying in the background and never bucking the establishment. His health, which he cared for assiduously the closer that Lewis approached retirement, held on long enough for Boyle to be in position when Lewis stepped down. And his luck carried Boyle over the body of another man who died in the presidency of the union.

Lewis, by 1952, felt he had accomplished his life's work. He had muscled his way into the union presidency in 1920, fought off other challengers over the years, set himself up as a demigod at union headquarters in the 1930s (when he purchased the six-story building from a private club), and even made himself a hero to much of the rest of the labor movement, against whose grain he rubbed in the 1940s. After the Second World War, the decline of coal wiped out jobs in the industry, and Lewis, with the aid of younger men like Boyle and Yablonski, came up with contracts that preserved more than 100,000 jobs where there had once been 400,000. Lewis also fought to develop the Welfare and Retirement Fund, financed eventually by the forty-cent-a-ton royalty on each ton of union-mined coal, which provided at least some hospital care and modest pension for a growing number of retired miners. Paradoxically, the more that coal-mine jobs disappeared, the more productivity grew among coal miners, because of mechanization, so that in the twenty years between 1945 and 1965 output per man tripled, to around seventeen tons a day.

The result was that the United Mine Workers, despite declining membership, became a wealthy union, and when Lewis approached his eightieth birthday in 1960, he saw to it that each of the top international officers would be able to retire on a pension amounting to full pay—in the case of the president, $50,000 a year. Then he named his successor, Thomas Kennedy, a former lieutenant governor of Pennsylvania who was, however, gravely ill. Boyle became vice president, ran much of the union's day-to-day affairs, and when Kennedy died on January 21, 1963, Tony Boyle became the first UMW president from west of the Mississippi.

He was born in Bald Butte, Montana, though the exact year was a matter of confusion, or possibly obfuscation, until Boyle testified under oath about it in 1974. On assuming the presidency, he said his birthday was December 1, 1907, making him fifty-six. In several editions of *Who's Who in America* during the 1960s, he gave his birth year as 1904, making him fifty-nine on assuming the presidency and sixty-five at the time of the 1969 election. He swore under oath later that he was really born in

1901, meaning he was past sixty when he became UMW president and sixty-seven when he sought reelection.

He was the son of James and Catherine Mallin Boyle, and often liked to point out that his father began work in the mines of England at the age of nine. Tony Boyle himself worked his way up from coal mines in Montana, where he was a UMW district president, to Washington headquarters in 1948.

Boyle was often called a troubleshooter for John L. Lewis, but the young assistant to the legendary president stayed in the background. In 1952, however, Boyle was named in a suit filed by a UMW worker in Wise, Virginia. Charles Minton claimed that he had been ordered to murder two coal operators, and the orders, he said, came from Tony Boyle. Minton sued for $350,000, claiming he had been fired and blacklisted for refusing to carry out the orders, although, he asserted, he had dynamited an electrical substation owned by a coal company. As a result of Minton's suit, a number of coal companies sued the union for $1 million, but all of the suits, including Minton's, were settled out of court, and the records disappeared from the courthouse in Virginia.

As he grew older, Boyle took to dyeing his thinning hair black and occasionally wearing makeup that obscured the wrinkles on his face. He walked erect, springing on the balls of his feet and occasionally reeling like a merchant seaman, and sometimes he held up his right hand to show the missing little finger, which he said was the victim of a mine accident in his youth.

Fully a year before the 1964 international union elections, Boyle began to make preparations for a run for a full five-year term. The union and the Bituminous Coal Operators Association had signed an open-ended contract in 1958, with no expiration date, and Boyle saw that to reopen it in 1964 would help provide him with political strength in the union. He helped negotiate a new two-year contract that provided a dollar-a-day raise in each of two years of the pact; a two-week vacation with $225 pay provided, and there were also seven holidays providing for double-time. But an ominous note, at least so far as Boyle's increasingly comfortable relationship with the coal industry was concerned, was a provision that the operators could require the men to work a seventh day in a week: at double-time, of course. Small wonder, then, that in negotiating his first UMW contract, Boyle took pride in stating that it was the fifth contract in fourteen years without a major work stoppage in the coal industry. The coal-company bosses could give similar prideful assurances to their stockholders.

Moreover, Boyle was fortunate to have the union election of 1964 coincide with a year for an international convention. The elections were normally held every five years, the conventions every four. The convention that fall was the launching pad for Boyle's first full term as union president. It was held in Miami Beach, hundreds of miles from the nearest coal mine, and there Boyle began to consolidate his power. The soft-coal contract behind him, he pointed to the gains miners had made under his leadership, and looked to the day when wages would go even higher, perhaps to fifty dollars a day. He solidified his control over the union's districts, slipping through a provision that in future elections challengers would require nominations of fifty locals, instead of five, to get on the ballot. At the union election in December that year, Boyle was easily chosen for a five-year term, over the token opposition of a neighbor of Yablonski's, Steve "Cadillac" Kochis. Now Boyle could begin acting like John L. Lewis.

First, Boyle tightened his hold over the union's twenty-four districts (twenty-two in the U.S., two in Canada) by continuing in office the men who showed loyalty to him—such as District 19's financial secretary, Albert Pass, and its president, William Turnblazer. Pass was the tough one; Turnblazer, whose father had been District 19 president, was pliable. The rank-and-file members could not choose their district officers in most of the districts, and Boyle recognized the advantages of that to the incumbent leaders. He was not about to grant what came to be known as "autonomy"; instead, the districts were to remain as

John L. Lewis had fashioned them, "provisional trusteeships." Autonomy—that is, democratic election of district officers— became a dirty word in the UMW lexicon. Even though the Justice Department, in 1964, filed suit to end the practice of appointed officers, Boyle did not regard the legal challenge seriously. As the 1960s passed without any apparent movement on the government suit, Boyle became even less concerned about the threat of autonomy.

Another Boyle tactic was to win the approval of the working miners, who constituted more than half of the membership. For many miners, even as little as ten years after the amalgamation of organized labor in 1955, working in a coal mine was a feudal, backward existence. Their basic daily wage in 1964 was $24.25. Boyle managed to improve that to thirty-five dollars by the year 1971. They had few paid holidays; one of them being April 1, the anniversary of the eight-hour day, which the union had fought for at the turn of the century. Boyle saw to it that a few holidays were added and that pensions were improved modestly, and in 1966 he negotiated a thirty-month contract (which would conveniently expire a year before the 1969 election); it provided an hourly rate that was considered well above the industrial average in America.

But because almost all of the nation's coal miners were situated far from the union's headquarters in Washington, the less obvious tactics of the Boyle administration did not penetrate their thinking until near the end of Boyle's regime. Few knew that the Boyle administration spent $68,894 over a five-year period to maintain its international secretary-treasurer in a two-room suite at the Sheraton-Carlton Hotel in Washington. They read the unbridled praise for Boyle in the pages of the UMW *Journal* (dissenting letters to the editor were not printed), but few were aware of the three Cadillac limousines purchased for the top officers. The miners looked forward to two weeks a year away from the underground hell, but staff officers got four weeks' vacation.

Every coal miner knew someone who had been killed—over

100,000 have perished in the nation's coal mines in this century alone—but all they could hear from Tony Boyle were expressions of sadness and frequently reiterated statements that coal mining was inherently dangerous. In 1973, Boyle's successor, Arnold Miller, himself a working miner through most of Boyle's administration, called such fatalism a "myth." "Last July," Miller said, "nine coal miners died in a fire at Consolidation Coal's Blacksville Number One mine near Fairmont, West Virginia. They didn't die because coal mining is dangerous work. They died because Consolidation Coal Company violated the law."

Such expressions of outrage against the companies and the lax observance of safety regulations seldom came from President Boyle, because another method by which he maintained his power was to stay on good terms with what should have been his natural opponents, the leaders of the coal industry. Although underlings like Albert Pass talked tough on union matters, ranging District 19 to try to organize—or give the appearance of trying to organize—thousands of nonunion miners, Boyle always maintained close relationships with the captains of a supposedly dying industry. (Actually, despite the attrition of hundreds of thousands of jobs, the annual tonnage produced in the U.S. declined very little over a twenty-year period.) Boyle's leadership always argued that coal was in a decline, that the union had to take that into consideration before striking, but there was Tony Boyle, riding his chauffeured limousine, striving to reach what was considered the Nirvana of coal-mine wages—the magical fifty dollars a day. (Miners didn't achieve that pinnacle until 1974, and then only about a third of the most highly skilled qualified.)

Boyle's cooperation with the industry was never so evident as on the day when he arrived at Farmington, West Virginia, when seventy-eight men were trapped in the No. 9 mine of Consolidation Coal. Farmington is only twenty miles away from Monongah, West Virginia, where 361 men were killed in 1907 in the worst mining disaster in U.S. mining history. On the afternoon of November 22, 1968, Boyle walked into a concrete-block room at the company store in Farmington and faced more than a score of newspaper reporters, television cameramen, and still photographers. The cameras began rolling the moment he entered the room, and some of the reporters noted that President Boyle never removed his gray felt hat. His words went over a public-address system that was heard in the main part of the store by the women who were shortly to be declared the widows of the men trapped in the No. 9 mine. After expressing his sympathy, Boyle said, "The press should recognize in this particular instance the cooperation that has been extended by all parties. . . . I came down here today not to give orders as to how the work should be conducted, but more to make a showing here today in behalf of the cooperation."

Cooperation! To some in Boyle's audience that crisp November day, it seemed strange that the president of the big union put cooperation at the head of his priorities. Boyle elaborated with any prodding from the press:

"This happens to be, in my judgment as president of the United Mine Workers of America, one of the better companies, as far as cooperation and safety is concerned, to work with. It's a sad commentary that this thing had to happen anywhere, but more especially here. I'm grieved about it, I know everyone else is shaken about it. It was physically impossible for me to be here yesterday, or I'd have been here yesterday. I sent my safety director and suggested the Bureau of Mines get some people down here. I share the grief is all I can say at this time, because I'm shaken, too. I lost relatives, personally, relatives of my own, in explosions; I know what it is to be in an explosion. I've gone through several of them. And as long as we mine coal, there's always this inherent danger in the mining of coal. And necessary precautions, of course, compliance with all the laws both state and federal, must be complied with.

"I have no idea what set this explosion off. I don't think anyone else has. That will be determined when we make the investigation. But I can assure you, knowing the company offi-

cials as well as I do, that everything will be done to reveal to
the public and the mine workers' union, and we'll insist on it
being done, what caused this explosion, in an effort to prevent
future explosions of this nature."

The Farmington tragedy showed Boyle for what he was—an
insensitive labor leader who knew, and cared, little for the men
he led. In that moment of truth in the company store, when he
didn't even take his hat off out of respect to the agonizing
widows outside, he showed his true colors, and the effect was
not lost on the men in the nation's mines. Work stoppages began
soon after, and later there were demonstrations by hundreds of
West Virginia miners seeking what their union could not give—
compensation for the ravages of disease, meaningful insurance
for their widows, hospital benefits that wouldn't run out after
four years of disability, and most important, a voice in their own
destinies. In short, the seeds of democracy were planted in the
United Mine Workers in the ashes of Farmington, West Virginia, in November 1968.

A little-noticed action at the union convention in September
of that year probably played at least an equal role in the demise
of Tony Boyle. Jock Yablonski saw in close-up what the administration of Tony Boyle was doing to the UMW, and he
came away torn between loyalty to his leadership and the welfare of the rank and file. At Denver in 1968, Yablonski learned
that the two were incompatible.

One issue at the 1968 convention was the role of district
officers of the union. Yablonski was then international executive
board member for District 5, headquartered in Pittsburgh. Unlike most of the districts, Yablonski's enjoyed autonomy—that
is, the members elected their district president and international
board member.

Yablonski had been removed by Boyle in 1966 as district
president, allegedly for making shady deals with coal operators.
Actually, his supporters said, he was removed because he was
a threat to Boyle. The only post Yablonski then retained was

his IEB membership. But that term would expire in 1970, and if Yablonski lost it, he would be out of a union job.

Boyle's supporters say that at the convention of 1968, Yablonski "tried to put over a real sneak maneuver." The convention decided to elect officers of "provisional" districts to a five-year term, then and there. Those terms would expire in 1973. But Yablonski did not come from a provisional district. According to the Boyle camp, this is what Yablonski tried to do:

"Yablonski pleaded with UMWA president W. A. Boyle to have his [Yablonski's] name presented with the others, so that Yablonski could be elected by the convention and have his term expire in 1973 instead of 1970.

"President Boyle told Yablonski that he could not permit violation of the International and District Constitutions and that Yablonski's request also would violate federal law. Boyle would not permit Yablonski to go ahead with his scheme."

The story was put out in a lengthy union pamphlet that was rushed into print less than a month after Yablonski announced his candidacy against Boyle. Whether the story is true is lost in the murky history of the United Mine Workers. But it does demonstrate the lengths to which the Boyle forces went to oppose the candidacy of Jock Yablonski.

"Friends, associates and supporters" of Tony Boyle published scurrilous attacks on Yablonski that year. They pointed out correctly that he was a loyal supporter of Boyle as late as twenty-five days before he announced his candidacy, but they also called Yablonski a "shakedown" artist, a convicted thief (which he had been, in 1930, at the age of twenty), a hypocrite, and a "loudmouth." He was a "traitor" (supposedly because of praise from the publication of the Communist party); an "informer" (for having given derogatory information on the union to Ralph Nader); a "bigot" (because of Yablonski opposition years before to a Jewish candidate for a local judgeship); and a "child deserter" (because of a court order, in 1936, to pay his first wife support for young Ken Yablonski).

The "friends, associates and supporters" of Tony Boyle also

published a wholly undocumented story about Jock Yablonski
and John L. Lewis, wherein Lewis was supposed to have told
Yablonski on the eve of Lewis's retirement: "As for you, no man
who ever wore numbers across his chest will ever be president
of this union. Remember that!" (The "story" was headed: "No.
24786 Shall Not Be UMWA President.")

And the anonymous "friends, associates and supporters" of
Tony Boyle sounded strangely like Albert Pass at the June 23
IEB meeting ("President Boyle, we are with you") when they
declared from behind their unidentified "Election Bulletin":

"The American coal miners will not be fooled despite the
dirty work that has been done. The members of the United Mine
Workers of America will stop 'The Informer Yablonski' in his
muddy tracks. The members of the UMWA have done it before.
We shall do it to Yablonski."

Did Tony Boyle sanction this nonsense? Was he so hungry
for victory, so covetous of the shoes of the great John L., so
contemptuous of the "outsiders" calling for democracy in his
union, that he sanctioned the atmosphere that led to the murder
of one man and two women? In the weeks after the election,
Boyle's actions provided no clear answer.

As he liked to point out years later, Boyle cooperated fully
with the FBI, the Justice Department, and the Labor Department. Within days after the Yablonski bodies were found in
Clarksville, two FBI agents were in Boyle's office in Washington, questioning the union president for more than an hour.
Confident that there were no secrets to hide in the union records, Boyle turned over the files of the United Mine Workers
to agents of the Justice Department. Every scrap of paper, every
receipt and canceled check, he gave to the government men,
confident in the knowledge that there would be nothing embarrassing to turn up. It was all in the hands of the lawyers, Boyle
liked to say, and he had full confidence in the union's legal

department, headed by his shrewd friend, Ed Carey. Carey became Boyle's chief spokesman on the murder case, and said time after time that there was no connection with the union leadership.

Nor was Boyle bothered by the continuing legal assault on the union by Yablonski's supporters. Who were they? he asked. Could Mike Trbovich or Chip Yablonski negotiate with a coal operator? The courts would get that one, too, and Boyle was satisfied he could withstand the annoying legal jabs of Yablonski's attorney, Joe Rauh. Boyle had had his fights with Rauh before, and he could handle that man who, Boyle said, dictated policy to the *Washington Post.*

In short, during 1970, Boyle acted like the president of a major union who fully intended to stay in power for the balance of his five-year term. The rank and file had overwhelmingly elected him, he reasoned, and they weren't going to turn their backs on Tony Boyle. And nobody in the ranks of other union leaderships said otherwise.

"Tony Boyle," he would say in his accustomed third person, "is doin' fine. Tony Boyle is not a quitter."

Boyle, of course, guessed wrong on the union legal case.

The three Yablonski bodies were no sooner in their graves than the legal fights began. All the way up to the Supreme Court went Mike Trbovich, Jock's long-time neighbor, and Rauh. The court granted Trbovich standing as a plaintiff against the union. In the District of Columbia Federal Court, Judge Bryant ruled against Boyle, ordering a new election in 1972. The government moved quickly on the "autonomy" case, and another judge ruled that the rank and file had the right to elect their district leaders; gone was Boyle's power to handpick the union officials who handled everyday grievances of miners.

He guessed wrong, too, on the government's Corrupt Practices Act case against him—and he was given a five-year sentence in 1972 for his illegal union contributions to political campaigns. Boyle appealed that case, too, but the fire was going out of his voice just as surely as the power was being wrested from his wrinkled hands.

He had some grittiness left, though. In March of 1973, he was out of office, defeated in the rerun by the forces of Arnold Miller, but he flew to Erie to testify on behalf of William Prater. It took guts, and the action began even as his plane from Washington landed.

It was 7:30 P.M., and by coincidence, Jock's son Ken was at the Erie airport to see off Joe Rauh, who had finished testifying. Ken had a drink, then recognized some newsmen and photographers waiting in the lobby of the tiny airport.

"What's going on?" Ken asked.

He was told that they were waiting for Tony Boyle.

Ken decided to stick around. The plane from Washington was due in an hour.

"I want to see the man who murdered my father," Ken said. "I want to look the bastard in the eye."

When Boyle arrived, he marched confidently through the single gate at the airport. A sheriff's car was waiting outside. Between Boyle and the terminal exit were a dozen television cameras, an equal number of reporters, a crowd of spectators attracted by the newsmen—and at curbside near the sheriff's car, Ken Yablonski.

The photographers back-pedaled as the reporters fired questions at Boyle. His smile never left his face and he never broke stride as he marched the fifty feet to the exit. No, said Boyle, he knew nothing about the Yablonski murders. No, he said, they was not connected with the union. Yes, he was going to testify fully and completely.

At the curb outside, Ken Yablonski spotted the short springy-stepped man coming toward the sheriff's car. "There's the bastard that killed my father!" Ken yelled. "And they're giving him an escort!"

Boyle was hustled into the car and disappeared into the night, showing no sign that he had heard Ken Yablonski's words.

His testimony, of course, didn't help William Prater. Prater was convicted and then confessed a week after his trial. And Boyle's testimony was contradicted by William Turnblazer, the slight, timid lawyer who was president of the union's District 19. Poor William Turnblazer. His father had served the union for twenty-five years as District 19 president, and he had a brother named after John L. Lewis. Bill himself had worked his way up from the Tennessee hill country to a law degree, and now in Erie he was confessing that he had perjured himself on behalf of Albert Pass and Tony Boyle.

Bill Turnblazer could always be depended upon to follow orders; of that Tony Boyle was sure. But the convictions of Prater and then Pass in the summer of 1973 created an overwhelming pressure on Bill Turnblazer. The FBI men from Knoxville came around so often to his office in Middlesboro, Kentucky, that Turnblazer found it hard to concentrate on his work as District 19 president. Finally, he decided to tell all he knew about the Yablonski murders—he hadn't told it all yet. By August, he was ready to put down in writing the story that would seal the fate of Tony Boyle.

12

Back to the Beginning

THE FEDERAL BUREAU OF INVESTIGATION requires that its agents be schooled in at least one of two fields —accounting or the law. The nation's top law-enforcement agency thereby recognizes that money and illegal activities are inseparable. Although the FBI's exploits have been dramatized sometimes to the point of embarrassment, the plain fact is that weeks and months, sometimes years, of painstaking drudgery precede a major arrest. In real life, most of an agent's work is as glamorous as an account sheet or a law-school text.

In the summer of 1973, the FBI needed no prodding to step up the pace of its ongoing probe of the Yablonski murders. The impending arrest of Tony Boyle seemed to be the logical conclusion of the case, because Prosecutor Sprague had virtually promised, after Albert Pass's trial, that Boyle would be charged with the three killings. But the FBI had another incentive that summer: the stain of the Watergate scandals began to touch the FBI itself. Therefore, some agents looked at the Yablonski murder case, and proof of Tony Boyle's role in it, as a morale builder for the hitherto incorruptible G-men.

In Knoxville, Tennessee, in early July of 1973, FBI Agent Henry Quinn and his boss, Special Agent Wallace Estil, began reviewing once more a sheaf of files on United Mine Workers District 19. Now they looked at the fat collection of material in the light of Albert Pass's conviction in Erie. Pass indicated through his attorney that the government could not expect any cooperation from him, despite his concern for his wife and invalid daughter in Kentucky.

The focus of the investigators' attention turned toward William Turnblazer, who despite his admitted perjury was still president of District 19. Turnblazer's testimony had been useful at the trial of William Prater, but the FBI men now felt that the quiet lawyer and union official had more to tell them. Indeed, they concluded, if anyone was to implicate Tony Boyle in the Yablonski murders, it would *have* to be Turnblazer.

The two agents made several visits to Turnblazer's union office in Middlesboro, Kentucky—the same office he once shared with the real boss of District 19, Albert Pass—and soon Turnblazer began visiting Knoxville. His interrogators picked up the story from where Turnblazer had left it at Prater's trial— how he had lied to grand juries, and how he had known there was no such outfit as the Research and Information Committee. At Prater's trial, however, Turnblazer had denied taking part in any murder conspiracy.

The pressures on Turnblazer became enormous. Not only were the government agents bearing down on him, holding in reserve such charges as perjury, embezzlement, and possibly conspiracy to commit murder; within the United Mine Workers, the new administration of Arnold Miller was going to hold union elections, in which case Turnblazer might lose his union job. And he knew he could be disbarred as a lawyer.

He had always been a timid man, and despite his law degree a helpless man, powerless before the infamous forces that ran the United Mine Workers during Tony Boyle's administration. Even with Boyle's departure, the long habit of subservience was too ingrained in William Turnblazer for him to change his personality in his middle fifties. Turnblazer feared what might happen to him or his family should he talk. Such was the awesome power of the old union in Appalachia.

But under repeated questioning by the FBI, Turnblazer finally broke and told all he knew. He was not relieved by his

confession; he was still frightened, for he knew that he would
have to testify again in a court of law. He signed a thirty-four
page statement in which he described Boyle as saying in the
presence of himself and Albert Pass that "Yablonski ought to
be killed or done away with." The key element in the murder
plot—the instigation of Yablonski's killing by Boyle—was all
the prosecution needed to proceed against the former union
president. Turnblazer signed his statement on August 23, 1973.
Two weeks later, the FBI moved to arrest Tony Boyle for the
murders of Joseph, Margaret, and Charlotte Yablonski.

Boyle was taken into custody three days after Labor Day.
Sprague ordered that Turnblazer be taken to federal court in
Pittsburgh, to enter his confession and to pave the way for
federal charges against Boyle. The federal allegations—depriving a union member of his civil rights—were enough to insure
that Boyle would be brought to Pennsylvania without extradition proceedings.

But it was murder one that Sprague was going to try to pin
on Boyle, and so he arranged an almost cloak-and-dagger proceeding the night before Boyle's arrest and Turnblazer's court
appearance. Pennsylvania state trooper Elmer Schifko, who had
been among the first lawmen to find the Yablonski bodies, went
in secrecy before a Washington County judge. It was nearly
11:00 P.M. when Schifko swore out a murder warrant against
Boyle, charging him with conspiring with all the eight other
defendants in the case, adding in the precise legal language of
the complaint that "W.A. 'Tony' Boyle did feloniously, wilfully,
deliberately, with premeditation and with malice aforethought
murder Joseph Albert 'Jock' Yablonski, Margaret Rita Yablonski and Charlotte Jean Yablonski."

A three-page attachment to Elmer Schifko's complaint
spelled out details that were based largely on Turnblazer's
confession:

—That on June 23, 1969, Boyle "sought out and spoke pri-

vately with Albert Edward Pass and William Jenkins Turnblazer inside the national headquarters of the United Mine
Workers of America in Washington, D.C. . . . At this private
meeting, Boyle initiated and instigated a plan to assassinate and
murder Joseph Albert 'Jock' Yablonski."

—That Boyle told Pass and Turnblazer "Yablonski ought
to be killed or done away with."

—That Pass volunteered the services of District 19 and
"stated that District 19 would take care of it . . . Boyle stating
that he was in agreement."

—That $20,000 was obtained from the union treasury to pay
for the assassination—in effect, embezzlement of union funds
to cover a contract for murder.

On the morning of September 6, 1973, Sprague met a group
of news reporters in his office at Philadelphia's City Hall, where
he had invited them for an important announcement. He waited
half an hour for a call from Pittsburgh—word that Turnblazer
had entered his guilty plea—and then for another call from
Washington bringing the news that Boyle was under arrest.
Sprague did not gloat, or even smile, as he announced that he
expected to prosecute Boyle after the turn of the new year. "This
will be the end of the case," Sprague added. "We are back at
the beginning."

In Washington, D.C., at about 10:30 that morning, Tony
Boyle was greeted by a host of photographers and reporters
outside his brick home. He knew something was up but he
offered no statements. He went downtown to give a deposition
on behalf of his former union general counsel, Edward L. Carey.

That session was underway when two FBI men arrived. One
of them served Boyle with the papers. Then they escorted Boyle
out of the office. Among those left behind was Chip Yablonski,
the union's new general counsel. He didn't seem surprised at
the dramatic arrest of the man alleged to have instigated the
murder of his father.

Boyle seemed calm as he was taken to the Federal Court-house in Washington. He told pursuing reporters: "I don't know what this is all about."

Boyle pleaded not guilty to a federal charge of conspiring to deprive Yablonski of his civil rights, and told reporters later: "He conspired as much as I did. He campaigned the same way I did."

Bond for Boyle was set at $50,000. Released, he called the charges "ridiculous." "I never expected this was going to come through. I had no forewarning," he said.

He was held for a hearing on September 25, and returned to his home to map legal strategy.

In Philadelphia, Sprague began lining up witnesses in the expectation that Boyle, like the other defendants in the case, would face state murder charges first.

But Sprague reckoned without the desperation of his quarry. On the evening of September 24, 1973, a day before he was to attend a hearing on his removal to Pennsylvania, Tony Boyle played his last card against the onrushing wheel of justice. He was talking in his living room that night with an old friend, Charles "Timer" Moses, a tall silver-haired Montana criminal lawyer who had seldom come to the East, much less argued cases in eastern courts. Boyle wanted Moses to defend him. They discussed Tony's chances of beating the rap.

Around eleven o'clock, Boyle excused himself and went upstairs. Moments later, a thump was heard and then a cry. Boyle's personal physician was called, and Boyle was rushed to George Washington University Hospital. After midnight, the official word was put out to newsmen that Tony Boyle had suffered a stroke.

Richard Sprague didn't believe it. He got in touch with the Justice Department and suggested that men be sent to the hospital to guard Boyle, and that his medical records be immediately impounded.

In short order, the true story came out: Early that evening

Boyle had taken more than a hundred sleeping pills, in an apparent attempt to kill himself. To this day, Sprague tends to doubt that Boyle's intent was suicide. More likely, Sprague reasons, Boyle intended to make himself unavailable for his date with justice.

Boyle's illness did push back the timetable for his trial in Pennsylvania. As he lay recovering, the prosecution team fought off legal moves by Boyle's lawyers. They attempted to get the federal charges tried first, in hopes that an acquittal would make it impossible ever to try Boyle on state murder charges. But, as in previous cases in the Yablonski murders, the federal courts deferred to the state courts, with the murder case being allowed to take precedence over federal conspiracy charges.

It took nearly three months for Boyle to recover, and he still appeared woozy and distracted when federal marshals came for him on December 20, 1973. Their assignment was to take Boyle to Pennsylvania to be formally charged with murder. However, in a guarded hospital suite, Boyle had a fainting spell, and his trip to Washington County, Pennsylvania, was put off for a day.

The trip to Pennsylvania was, for Boyle, a stopover on his way to jail. The Supreme Court had refused to hear his appeal of his conviction for misusing union funds, and he had been sentenced to three years in a federal prison. Now he was to begin that sentence, at a federal center for medical prisoners in Springfield, Missouri.

First Boyle was flown to western Pennsylvania. He refused to put on street clothes, so the federal marshals let him wear his green hospital pajamas, a blanket wrapped around him against the snow and wind.

The plane went to Pittsburgh, where Boyle was transferred to a car that drove through a blinding snowstorm to the Washington County Courthouse. As Boyle was wheeled into Judge Sweet's courtroom, there sat Kenneth Yablonski and his uncle Edward. There, too, was the special prosecutor, who could scarcely hide his annoyance that Boyle's lawyer, Moses, was unable to appear. Moses had told the judge over the telephone that he was unable to get a plane out of Washington, but Sprague said he had checked, and found there were empty seats.

W.A. Boyle looked like a completely broken man—his hair, no longer dyed, tangled by the wind; his face seemingly oblivious of what was happening; his gnarled hands clutching at the blanket around his chest. The wheelchair seemed to belie the fact that only thirteen months earlier he had campaigned vigorously for reelection as head of one of the nation's largest labor organizations. Outside on Main Street, the Christmas lights were strung and bells were chiming, while Boyle sat before the bar of Courtroom Number One, accused as a common criminal.

The arraignment lasted only ten minutes, and was routine, with Boyle uttering a barely audible not guilty plea. Judge Sweet set January 28 for the trial, but most of the lawyers on hand concluded that that deadline would never be met.

Judge Sweet took the occasion to lecture Boyle on the conduct of one of his attorneys, Plato Cacheris, whom he had seen on television a few days earlier pleading for mercy for the seventy-two-year-old defendant. Sweet admonished Boyle: "We have a tradition for hard-nosed, but even-handed, justice here. You will be tried on the law and evidence and not in a court of public opinion."

Boyle listened with a blank stare.

When the arraignment was over, the federal agents took Boyle to a plane, along with a doctor and a nurse, and he was transferred to Missouri. In the eyes of some observers, Boyle didn't look like a man who was too sick to stand trial. Almost certainly, however, it looked as if the trial of Tony Boyle would have to be taken out of Washington County, where even a ten-minute arraignment in the case was enough to generate enormous publicity.

Shortly before the spring of 1974, the defense and prosecution agreed to a trial outside Washington County. To Sprague's delight, the Pennsylvania Supreme Court chose Delaware

County, which adjoins Philadelphia in the southeastern part of the state. Having the trial so close to home, where he was well known and respected, was a major victory for Sprague. In 1971, the state had named him a special prosecutor to investigate alleged corruption in Delaware County, but at the time of Boyle's trial, Sprague had not yet issued a report on his findings. The county, rock-ribbed Republican since the Civil War, had a long history of unproved official corruption, but all Sprague had done in his investigation was to uncover some minor figures. If justice is not blind to politics, then Sprague certainly wielded a major weapon in having the Boyle trial shifted to Delaware County.

Sprague found another weapon to hold over the head of Boyle's chief attorney, Charles Moses. Before the jury was to be chosen, Moses told a newspaper reporter about the results of a lie-detector test administered to Boyle. Moses said the test results "were entirely favorable to the defendant." Furious at this apparent breach of courtroom ethics, Sprague brought the story to the attention of the Delaware County Court. A judge, equally angry, called Moses into private session, threatened him with contempt charges, then held the matter over until the end of Boyle's trial. For the rest of his stay in Delaware County, Moses never said another word to a reporter.

The site for Boyle's murder trial was a quiet suburban courthouse in the town of Media, fifteen miles southwest of Philadelphia. Once again, strict security governed the proceedings: Everyone entering the courtroom was searched, doors were locked during testimony, and no one entered without a special pass.

The judge was a stern-faced veteran of Republican county politics named Francis J. Catania. He was every bit as harsh as Washington County's Judge Sweet, but without Sweet's leavening of wit. Though seemingly impartial, Catania occasionally showed impatience with the courtroom habits of defense attorney Moses, who tended to use ten words where two would do.

Testimony got under way on April 1—ironically, the UMW union holiday marking the anniversary of the eight-hour working day. Sprague was determined to schedule his witnesses in such fashion as to get the trial over in less than two weeks. Easter was a fortnight away, and Sprague realized that certain holidays are not auspicious for a jury to be deliberating a man's fate.

The jury of nine men and three women had taken five days to complete. Tony Boyle was lodged at a nearby hospital, under heavy guard. He was able to walk into and out of the courthouse, and as the trial progressed, his color and strength appeared to improve. He developed a daily ritual of waving at three of his family members—his wife Ethel, his daughter Antoinette, and his brother Richard—as he entered the courtroom. The two women offered a strange picture as they sat on the second row: Both wore a chalky white makeup that made their faces look like ghosts', and both had their hair dyed a flaming orange. Throughout the trial the two women would comment on the proceedings, whispering frequent disagreements with the judge's rulings, nodding approval when they were pleased by one of defense attorney Moses's tactics. Antoinette Boyle, a woman in her mid-forties, was a lawyer who had had a $40,000-a-year job on the union payroll in Montana, when her father was the president of the United Mine Workers. Richard Boyle had held a $25,000-a-year union post in Montana, but claimed to have been appointed long before his brother took over the top spot in the union. The Boyle family never so much as glanced at members of the Yablonski family, who sat several rows behind the prosecution table.

One person they did watch closely was Sprague. They snickered when Sprague came on strong with his opening address to the jury. Using a map of the eastern United States to drive home the massiveness of the state's investigation (which also gave him an opportunity to walk close to Boyle and point a finger at him), Sprague spoke for more than an hour, his deep voice carrying to the rear of the huge courtroom:

"You're gonna hear," Sprague told the jury, "the evidence which will show and indicate to you that this defendant sitting right here is the man that used money from the United Mine Workers, the sweat and the blood of the miners of America, to pay for murdering Jock Yablonski. . . .

"You're gonna hear how Jock Yablonski, Joseph Yablonski, had the guts, had the courage to try to unseat this defendant from the presidency of that union. And you're gonna hear how on May 29, 1969, Mr. Yablonski announced that he was going to run for the presidency of the United Mine Workers of America, and in so doing signed his own warrant of death at the hands of this defendant sitting right here."

Tony Boyle studied the pink walls of the courtroom, never flinching during Sprague's repeated finger-pointing at the defense table. The defense had a disadvantage: Moses spoke to the jurors just before lunchtime, and before his one-hour speech was over, some members of the jury could be seen squirming restlessly in their chairs or looking up at the courtroom clock.

Moses's opening was unorthodox, at least as far as Pennsylvania courts are concerned. The purpose of the opening speech is to tell the jury what sort of evidence each side will present. Instead, Moses began by giving a biography of himself—before a Sprague objection stopped it.

"I am a lawyer from Billings, Montana," said Moses. "I can tell you that Billings, Montana, is located one hundred and thirty miles northeast of Yellowstone Park, if that will help orient you in any way."

Because of Moses's frequent digressions, Sprague offered repeated objections—a rare procedure in opening speeches. The objections, in turn, led to sidebar conferences with the judge, out of the hearing of the jury. Sprague repeatedly told Judge Catania that Moses was not sticking to his agreement to describe testimony, but instead was presenting argument. The judge cautioned Moses several times, but the effect on the jurors seemed to be to distract attention from the substance of the defense

attorney's presentation. Good courtroom practice, like good
stagecraft, requires a sense of pace and momentum; Moses never
developed either. Even in playing his strongest point—that
Tony Boyle would testify in his own defense—Moses seemed
to squander his effectiveness by getting bogged down in Boyle's
biography:

"In connection with the testimony to be offered in this particular case, and the evidence to be produced from the stand,
Mr. Boyle will testify in this case. He will advise you and testify
from the stand that he is a man of seventy-two years of age, was
born in 1901, I think, in Montana, that he was raised in Bald
Butte, Montana, which is about thirty miles from Helena, which
is in the center of the state. . . ."

In a sharp, high-pitched voice, Moses spoke on well past the
noon hour. Stomachs were rumbling, the shades were drawn,
making the courtroom muggy, and Moses began to speak more
quickly. At the prosecution table, Sprague became increasingly
impatient, entered more objections, and finally told Judge Catania at a sidebar conference:

"Your Honor, may I say I have never heard a counselor
continue to violate rulings by the Court as I have heard Mr.
Moses do in this opening. I call upon this court to enforce its
rulings, because it is getting in my opinion kind of like a jack
in a jumping box, jack in some sort of a box, this jumping up
and down and coming here to get compliance with the court's
ruling."

Shortly after this demand by Sprague, Moses finished his
address to the jury. One waited in vain for some expression of
outrage that his client, long a respected national figure in the
labor movement, president of a major union for nearly a decade,
should be charged with murder. Instead, before the jurors hurried out to lunch, they heard Moses conclude: "The ultimate
issue that the jury will be called upon to decide in this case is
simply whether Mr. Boyle was responsible for these deaths. The
answer is No."

That afternoon, testimony began with Kenneth Yablonski and Paul Gilly. Sprague intended to have Gilly on the stand most of the afternoon, so that jurors would think about the murderer over night.

Boyle sat erect in his chair, pondering every word of Ken Yablonski's description of the murder scene, for this was the first time Boyle had heard the chilling account of the discovery of the bodies. Under Judge Catania's rules, the attorneys were required to sit at their tables while questioning witnesses. Sprague would have liked to approach Yablonski's son, in order to make the testimony more intimate. Uneasy off his feet, Sprague found a way to stand up now and then: whenever there were exhibits or photographs to show to the jury, he would ask the judge for permission to hand them over personally. It was as if the prosecutor needed some physical contact with the jurors.

Forced by the court's rule to sit at his table, Moses had to shout at Yablonski in a high-pitched voice:

"Was this your natural mother?"

Sprague: Objection, Your Honor.

The Court: Objection sustained.

Moses: Was this your natural sister?

Sprague: Objection!

The Court: Sustained.

Apparently shaken, Moses called for a sidebar discussion with the judge. There he argued that the question of Kenneth Yablonski's parentage "has been raised on the direct examination."

"That issue was not raised on direct examination," replied Judge Catania.

"He said it was his mother," Moses continued, "and I want to find out if it is his natural mother."

"In characterizing that woman as his mother," the judge said, "he is denoting that that is the person that he held in regard as his mother."

Red-faced, Moses returned to his table, said a few whispered words to Boyle, then requested another sidebar conference, leaving Kenneth Yablonski sitting baffled in the witness chair. This time, the defense attorney sought to introduce as evidence maps of two counties surrounding the murder home "so that his testimony will be clear." Sprague objected, and the judge again refused Moses's request. After a few more minutes of legal wrangling—"I might as well not cross-examine," Moses grumbled—the defense lawyer went back to his table, and now he was clearly flustered in his first cross-examination of the trial.

"Mr. Yablonski," he asked Kenneth, "when you went to the house and after you had discovered the death of your father, mother, and daughter, as you have described——"

"Sister!" Sprague shouted.

Kenneth Yablonski spent half an hour undergoing questioning on seemingly trivial issues raised by Moses—such items as the distance of the house from various towns, directions one would take on entering the house. The net effect, then, appeared to be that Moses was unnecessarily badgering a witness who had suffered a deep personal tragedy. Certainly it was difficult to see the pertinence of the kind of dog the Yablonskis owned.

As a contrast to Kenneth Yablonski's testimony, Sprague summoned Paul Gilly, the confessed killer. It was during his testimony that a scene straight out of Perry Mason shook the courtroom. Gilly had begun giving details of the murders and had identified Claude Vealey as one of his partners. Sprague asked that Aubran Martin be brought in so that the jurors could see the third triggerman.

Martin was screaming when he was led into the courtroom, handcuffed to a state policeman on both sides. Sprague asked Gilly to identify Martin. Martin began stomping one of his feet and swearing. Suddenly he whirled in the direction of Sprague, who was sitting with two assistants at the prosecution table. Before the police could subdue him, Martin spat viciously at Sprague, scoring a direct hit on the prosecutor's left shoulder.

Sprague's assistant, William Wolf, jumped up as if to clobber Martin, but Sprague restrained his colleague.

"Mr. Gilly," said Sprague coldly, "can you identify this person that has been brought here in the courtroom?"

Martin began shouting at the top of his voice.

"Your Honor," he yelled, "I've been kidnaped and brought here against my will and they won't let me contact my attorney or nothing!"

Sprague ignored the diatribe, as did the judge.

"Can you identify this person?" Sprague asked Gilly.

"Yes, sir."

"Who is that?"

By now, Martin was struggling with the two officers.

"I knew him as Buddy Martin," said Gilly.

"Is he the other person that went with you on this murder to Clarksville?"

"Yes, sir."

"Take him out," said Sprague, with contempt.

Martin began shrieking at Gilly:

"You are a lying mother fucker, too. That goddam redneck killed both!"

Sprague conceded to friends later that the Martin episode was a big plus for the prosecution.

Paul Gilly was the first witness to mention Boyle's name in connection with the Yablonski murders. During a lengthy cross-examination by Moses, Gilly discussed a meeting in William Prater's basement in Tennessee, the purpose of which was to decide how and where Yablonski would be killed. Also on hand, said Gilly, was his father-in-law Huddleston.

"They said if it was at all possible to make sure he was killed in Washington, D.C.," Gilly related.

"In other words," said Moses, "it was Mr. Prater and Mr. Huddleston that requested that he be killed in Washington, D.C.?"

"Yes, sir."

"It was not based on a request of any other person?"

"Yes, sir," said Gilly quietly.

"What other person?"

"Mr. Boyle."

Boyle's lawyer seemed stunned. "Pardon?" he said.

"Mr. Boyle," Gilly repeated.

"Was that a part of the discussion?"

"Yes, sir, Mr. Tony Boyle."

"I am sorry," said Moses, "I did not hear the last part?"

"He said Mr. Tony Boyle requested it," Gilly replied.

"So that at this conversation in Mr. Prater's basement he said that Mr. Boyle had requested that he be shot in Washington, D.C.?"

"Yes, sir," said the polite Gilly, almost inaudibly.

Moses then tried to show that Gilly was contradicting testimony he gave at an earlier trial that Albert Pass wanted the job done in Washington. Gilly acknowledged the discrepancy, then quietly asked the judge if he might explain.

"At this same conversation and at this same time," said Gilly, "Mr. Prater and Mr. Huddleston both said that Pass was handling this for Mr. Boyle, through District Nineteen."

No amount of rehearsal could have produced a better witness for the prosecution—Gilly, the soft-spoken killer who had decided to come clean after being sentenced to death in the electric chair.

The trial of Tony Boyle was going well for the prosecution. Sprague and several dozen police and expert witnesses had taken over an entire wing at a nearby Holiday Inn, and each night Sprague looked for ways to cut corners and save time. He decided not to put Silous Huddleston on the witness stand —with his advanced years and debilitating diseases, the old man was losing his memory as to dates and places. Sprague declined also to put Annette Gilly on the witness stand, because she could do little more than corroborate the stories of her husband and Claude Vealey. A host of police witnesses would testify, of course, about the details of the murders, and Kathy Rygle, now eighteen, would again relate her story of how she and her girl friend took down license numbers on the day three killers were in the Yablonski neighborhood. Nor would Sprague let most of the elderly miners testify about the kickback of money for the murders; he figured on parading them into the courtroom in small groups, to let the jury see the fear written on their faces.

That left two vital witnesses, William Prater and William Turnblazer, both District 19 officials who had had brief contacts with Tony Boyle. Sprague listened again to their stories at long prep sessions, and the prosecutor recognized again how each conveyed the awesomeness of a far-off power in Washington.

William Jackson Prater climbed into the witness box eagerly. Dressed in his neatly pressed green suit, his silver curly hair neatly brushed, he presented the picture of a reformed criminal who had also been well fed in a federal prison. He was deferential to Prosecutor Sprague and circumspect with defense attorney Moses. He readily identified Albert Pass, who was brought into the courtroom in a suit that appeared two sizes too big for him, as the man who ran District 19. He also identified ten of the pathetic old men, his former friends, whose signatures were used to cover up the murder money. And once more he was eloquent on the subject of why he had decided to tell the truth:

"I have a wife and seven children, and lying is against my principles. It has been. And I think you would have a hard time trying to find where I lied to the United Mine Workers or anybody. I was loyal to the union, I was loyal to people instructing me as to what to do. . . . Too many innocent people were being hurt and it was time that we started thinking about our families and the other people involved."

The new element in Prater's story was his account of what happened when Tony Boyle visited him before testifying at Prater's trial in Erie. The scene was the Erie county jail, about ten o'clock on the night of March 19, 1973.

"He [Boyle] told me to stick to my story," said Prater. "And, he says, even if you are convicted, stick to your story."

Throughout the long days of his trial, Boyle's health seemed to improve. He became more and more alert, he smiled more, and some of the old springiness seemed to return to his legs as he entered and left the courtroom. Occasionally he scrawled notes on a yellow pad, and when members or officials of the union testified he leaned forward, but did not acknowledge their presence. Arnold Miller, Boyle's successor as union president, took the witness stand briefly. Miller confirmed that Yablonski had never conceded his defeat by Boyle, and that the murdered union leader would have continued his legal fight against the Boyle administration. Miller looked at Boyle and Boyle looked at Miller, neither man flinching, and then the brief confrontation was over.

But it was during the testimony of William Jenkins Turnblazer that Boyle paid the greatest attention to the witness stand. Turnblazer, the former president of District 19, was Sprague's principal witness. The prosecutor called him to the stand late on a Monday. Sprague had several more witnesses, but he was determined to rest his case that day.

Turnblazer sat a bit stooped in the witness stand, hands clenched, his eyes seldom leaving the floor area between himself and the prosecutor. Under slow questioning by Sprague, Turnblazer quietly told what happened on the afternoon of June 23, 1969, at the United Mine Workers building in Washington.

"Mr. Turnblazer," Sprague asked, "were you present when the orders, the direction was given to assassinate Joseph Yablonski?"

A. Yes, sir.

Q. And who gave those orders?

A. Mr. Boyle.

Q. Do you see him here in this courtroom?

A. Yes, sir.

Q. Point him out.

A. Sitting at the defendant's table.

Turnblazer turned his head to the right ever so slightly, kept his body facing forward, then looked again at the front of the witness box, his face seemingly drawn by remorse or fear.

Turnblazer was asked about details of the 1969 meeting, which occurred less than a month after Yablonski had announced that he would run against Boyle for the union presidency.

Q. Now following that meeting of the executive board, is that when there was this meeting between this defendant, Pass, and yourself?

A. Yes, sir.

Q. And where was this meeting?

A. Just outside the board room in the hall.

Q. And what did this defendant then say, and who was he speaking to?

A. He was speaking to me and Mr. Pass.

Q. And what did this defendant say?

A. He said,"We are in a fight, we have got to kill Yablonski or take care of him."

Q. To kill Yablonski or take care of him? Was there any response by Pass?

A. Mr. Pass said if nobody else would kill him, District Nineteen would.

Q. And after Pass said if no one else will kill him, District Nineteen would, what did this defendant Boyle say?

A. As I recall, he said, "Fine."

That was the crux of the prosecution case, and Sprague paused, making sure Turnblazer's words had penetrated to every member of the jury.

Turnblazer gave no other details of the hallway meeting, and Sprague went on to question him about the Research and Information Committee, which Turnblazer said was a phony, set up by Albert Pass to cover up the $20,000 in union money for the killings.

"I said there's no way to convert that money without it

sticking out like a sore thumb," Turnblazer testified he told Pass. "He said that's the way it's got to be."

Turnblazer added that after the Yablonski murders, there were meetings and conversations between Boyle, Pass, and himself to mesh their stories for the FBI and grand juries. He said one such meeting took place when he sat beside Boyle on a plane taking them to a grand jury appearance in Pittsburgh.

Defense attorney Moses was unable to shake Turnblazer's story, though he got the witness to admit that the corridor meeting lasted only about a minute. He also admitted that this was the only first-hand knowledge he had of any participation by Boyle in the murder plot.

Over the strenuous objections of Moses, who argued that his client was tired and ill, Judge Catania allowed Sprague to continue his case into an evening session, and after three more witnesses, the prosecution finished. It was now past eight o'clock, Boyle was calling for his medication, and the defense would begin in a bit over twelve hours.

It was obvious that the chief defense witness was going to be Boyle himself. Even his own secretaries had testified against him, and his long-time closest associate was waiting in the wings to rebut parts of his testimony. Charles Moses summoned three prosecution witnesses on behalf of the defense—Silous Huddleston, David Brandenburg, and Annette Gilly—but he failed significantly to destroy the fabric of the prosecutor's presentation.

Now Boyle's name was called, and for a man of seventy-two who had suffered a humiliating election defeat, a three-year federal sentence, and a suicide attempt, he seemed to have a surprising reserve of strength. In the witness box he underwent forty-five minutes of friendly questioning by his lawyer. He coughed occasionally, twice reminded the judge that he was under medical care, but generally seemed to bear up well under the barrage of questions.

Moses developed the picture of a man who had worked in

the mines or on the miners' behalf for his entire adult life. Boyle portrayed himself as a good friend of Joseph Yablonski: "As the years went by, he and I became very close friends."

Asked how he had reacted to the discovery of the Yablonski bodies, Boyle testified: "After I heard the news that day, I became ill at my stomach, and I usually work fourteen, fifteen, sixteen hours a day. And I went home, I was sick."

In the spectators' section of the courtroom, the two Yablonski brothers showed surprise when Boyle stated that he suggested a $50,000 reward for the apprehension of the killers.

As Boyle sipped his water, cleared his throat, or fingered the Bible in front of him, it was difficult to believe that this wizened old man was the monster the prosecution had painted him. Boyle could not have appeared more dignified had he still been president of the United Mine Workers—which at times he seemed to believe he was, since he used the present tense in recounting his union activities. He would lean to his left, toward the jurors, and painstakingly explain what it meant to be head of a two-hundred-thousand-member union.

But Moses's task was not merely to present Boyle as an honest former labor leader. The objective was to shoot holes in the prosecution's contention that this sick old man played a role in the murders.

Regarding the alleged meeting with Albert Pass at the 1968 union convention in Denver, Boyle testified:

"He said, 'We cannot call them district organizers, district representatives, international representatives, or international organizers, because just as soon as word get out that these old men are representing the union, that they will be either beaten up, shot, and some of them have been threatened, will be threatened, would be killed.' He said, 'We will give them a different name.'

"I said, 'What do you mean by that?'

"He said, 'We will call it the Research and Information Committee.' "

It was the same story Boyle had told at the trial of William Prater a year earlier, and now Moses asked him about the June 23, 1969 meeting where Turnblazer said the three men agreed Yablonski should be killed. Boyle was generous with his details of a meeting that had occurred nearly four years earlier.

"I announced to the board meeting," he said, looking to the jury in his role as union president, "that there would be a meeting of the [district] presidents in my office, the district presidents and only the district presidents, in my office at three thirty that afternoon or thereabouts.

"And I left the main entrance; you would have to know the description of the hallway there. I left the main entrance of the board room, and the stairway is right there. And all of the men who were coming out of the board room were there. Mr. Budzanoski and Mr. Seddon grabbed me by the arm and said that they had to see me before the presidents' meeting. And I told them I didn't have time. And they insisted on seeing me, and they came down the stairway."

Q. Did you at any time after you left the meeting have any conversation with Albert Pass?

A. I did not.

Q. Did you at any time have any meeting or any conversation with William J. Turnblazer?

A. I did not.

Boyle also denied having talked with Turnblazer on a plane on his way to the grand jury in Pittsburgh. "I sat with the general counsel as I always do," said Boyle, directly contradicting Turnblazer's testimony that they sat next to each other and discussed the elderly miners who were beginning to talk to the FBI.

Boyle's account of his jailhouse meeting with William Prater in Erie was also completely opposite to the story told by Prater, who said Boyle had urged him to "stick to your story." Boyle claimed that it was Prater's lawyer who suggested the meeting, not Boyle, and that he told Prater: "I hope you stand up, you are going to be innocent of this thing. I said, 'It is my firm belief that the coal miners were not affected in any way.' "

Finally, there came a general denial by Boyle of the murder charges:

Q. Did you have anything to do with the killing of Joseph Yablonski, Margaret Yablonski, or Charlotte Yablonski?

A. Did I have anything to do with it?

Q. Yes, sir.

A. Absolutely not.

Q. Did you ever talk to Albert Pass or William Turnblazer and suggest to them that they kill Mr. Yablonski?

A. I certainly did not. To the contrary.

Moses completed his examination of his client. The judge called a ten-minute recess, and Prosecutor Sprague sat at his table, eager to begin. He knew how he was going to handle the witness—demolishing him by showing that he was a liar.

When the recess was over, Sprague began in his customary loud voice, confident, knowing that he had in reserve witnesses who could contradict Boyle on every major point. The prosecutor was also coming to the conclusion that his own key witness, Turnblazer, would stand up as a credible person. So off he went on a ninety-minute, uninterrupted cross-examination of Boyle that was marked by repetitiveness, angry tones from the prosecutor, and the fascinated attention of the jury:

Q. Mr. Boyle, you told this jury that the offer of the reward for the apprehension of the people who committed this horrible act and assassinated Jock Yablonski was your idea. Is that correct?

A. That is right.

Q. It was not and it is not a fact that your executive secretary Suzanne Richards suggested to you that a reward be posted and that the amount be a hundred thousand dollars?

A. I have no recollection of that, no, sir.

Q. You have no recollection of that?

A. No, sir.

Q. Did that happen?

A. No, not to my knowledge.

Q. And after Suzanne Richards made the recommendation to you that it be a hundred thousand dollars, you said, "Let's cut it down to fifty"?

A. I don't recall that, no, sir.

Q. Are you denying that happened?

A. Yes, sir, as near as I recall, that couldn't happen.

Q. It could not?

A. No, sir.

By this opening line of questioning and by the mention of Suzanne Richards's name, Sprague was exerting a pressure on Boyle it would be difficult to appreciate unless one were Boyle himself. Miss Richards, who is a lawyer, had been Boyle's most trusted assistant for two decades, and her role in the union became more and more important with Boyle's rise to power. The invocation of her name by Sprague was a signal to Boyle that even his closest associate stood ready to testify for the prosecution. And in fact she waited even at that moment in the prosecution's witness room.

In similar psychological fashion, Sprague played games with Boyle's memory, which had been so sharp and clear regarding the June 23 meeting:

Q. Now when was the executive board meeting prior to June twenty-third, 1969?

A. When was the meeting prior to the twenty-third? There was a meeting on, I believe, the first week of June of 1969.

Q. Do you remember what date?

A. I believe the meeting was, I know it was in the first part of the week of——

Q. Do you remember the date, is my question?

A. No, I do not.

Q. What time was that meeting over?

A. I don't recall.

Q. When you walked out of that meeting, who did you walk out with?

A. On June second or third.

Q. The prior meeting.

A. In all probability, I walked out with Secretary-Treasurer Owens, because I usually walked out with him.

Q. You usually walked out with him? Do you remember who you walked out with?

A. No, I do not.

Sprague then showed that Boyle could not remember details of the union meeting *after* June 23, until finally this exchange took place:

Q. All of a sudden in 1974, you can remember who you walked out of the meeting with on June twenty-third, 1969, is that right?

A. But you won't let me explain.

Q. Is that right?

Moses: May he explain.

Judge: After he answers the question, he may explain.

Sprague: Will you answer the question? Is that right?

A. Did I remember that, who walked out with me?

Q. Yes.

A. Yes, I remember . . .

Q. In other words, from June twenty-third, 1969, right up to today, it has always stayed in your mind who you walked out with on that meeting of June twenty-third, 1969?

A. If you will let me explain, I will tell you why.

Q. Is that right?

A. It remains with me because I remember it, yes, I remember it.

Sprague fired questions like bullets, abruptly switching subjects, suddenly zooming in on the jail meeting with Prater, which Boyle, confused, thought had occurred in 1972, when he was still union president.

"But you remember," Sprague interjected, "who you walked out of a meeting with back in 1969?"

"I have reason to remember it," said Boyle, and Sprague paused, surveying the jurors with his eyes. The entire panel, motionless, was looking at Boyle.

Sprague brought out that the two men Boyle said accompanied him from the 1969 meeting were friends of Boyle's and, moreover, that they had been convicted of embezzling union funds.

"When they were both convicted," Sprague asked, "did you keep them on the payroll?"

"Yes, sir," replied Boyle.

Out of a file of documents, Sprague then plucked a copy of the proceedings of the international executive board for late January 1970, the union hierarchy's first meeting after the Yablonski murders. Boyle was unable to say which officers he walked out with from that meeting: "I would have no reason." At the meeting, Sprague showed, Albert Pass received a standing ovation after his report on the work of District 19's "Research and Information Committee." The ovation, according to the minutes, was called for by Boyle.

The Research and Information Committee could now be read as a built-in coverup, laid out in the union's proceedings, but Boyle denied giving a copy of the minutes to Pass for transmission to Turnblazer.

"You are absolutely positive, Mr. Boyle," said Sprague, his voice increasing in volume, "that in no way did you handle any copy of these minutes to give to Mr. Pass to give to Mr. Turnblazer?"

"To the best of my recollection, no," answered Boyle.

Sprague rephrased the question four or five times more, and Boyle denied even so much as touching the minutes. Finally Sprague demanded: "And if your fingerprint happens to be on a copy of the minutes of January 22, 1970, you have no idea how it got there?"

"No, I would not," said Boyle confidently.

But one sensed that Richard Sprague would produce the fingerprint in court.

Although Boyle spent an hour and a half under the grueling queries of Sprague, he did not appear to be broken; but he did come across as a man of strange insensitivities. For example, he said he never looked into the question of the alleged kick-backs to the elderly miners while he was president of the union. Boyle squirmed under Sprague's probing for his reasons for not looking into the allegations, but Boyle refused to backtrack, giving the impression that such matters were beneath the attention of the head of the union.

Q. Weren't you interested in who caused these horrible deaths?

A. I certainly was, and I did more about it than any other individual, to try to apprehend the people that committed them.

Q. I'm sure you can apprehend them. . . . So what is the best way for you to find out whether there is a kickback? Isn't it for you, the president of the United Mine Workers of America, to find out what men, the names of those men, and call them in one by one and say to them, "Hey, fellows, did you have to kick back this money?"

A. That is a good statement at this time, but——

Q. You didn't think of that at that time?

A. No, that is a good statement now to make, yes, very good.

Q. Were you concerned with what you might hear from these men?

A. It never dawned on me that the men were kicking back.

Q. But you didn't want to make any attempt to find out what they would say, did you?

A. I had no way of doing that. I didn't know who was on the Research and Information Committee.

For a period of about ten minutes, Sprague and Boyle played cat and mouse over the question of Albert Pass's request for $20,000—the alleged murder payoff money—and though Boyle said over and over that union districts frequently requested money from Washington, he had to concede this was the first time such a money request went directly through himself. He implied that the details of the transaction were now hazy in his mind, adding: "But I have never sworn under oath, lied under oath."

"The jury will decide that, Mr. Boyle," Sprague shot back.

When the long cross-examination was over, neither Richard Sprague nor Tony Boyle showed any sign of exhaustion. Somewhere during his afternoon on the witness stand, Boyle seemed to have gained his second wind. He needed no assistance when he left the witness box for his return to the hospital. The Bible he had been fingering on the stand remained open to where Boyle had been reading.

Wednesday of that Holy Week brought a swift conclusion to testimony in *Commonwealth of Pennsylvania* vs. *W.A. Boyle.* The defense ended by presenting several men who were present at the June 23, 1969 meeting, and all testified that they saw no separate tête-à-tête involving Boyle, Pass, and Turnblazer.

For his rebuttal, Prosecutor Sprague called Boyle's long-time assistant, Suzanne Richards, to tell what she knew about the union group that flew to Pittsburgh for grand jury appearances. Looking directly at Boyle, she said Turnblazer sat next to Boyle on the flight, thereby directly contradicting her former boss's testimony that he sat with the union general counsel. William Prater's lawyer, H. David Rothman, testified that the jail meeting between Boyle and Prater was not at his own behest but at Boyle's, another contradiction. Chip Yablonski, now the general counsel of the union, contradicted Boyle's details about the physical layout of the Mine Workers building. Yablonski said it was not possible to leave the board room and go downstairs in the fashion described by Boyle.

As a *coup de grâce,* Sprague recalled Charles Groenthal, the FBI's top fingerprint expert, to identify a plastic-encased copy of the January 1970 minutes of the union meeting. Groenthal testified that the minutes were turned over to the FBI by Turnblazer and that a fingerprint belonging to Tony Boyle was found on the first page.

Groenthal had come prepared to demonstrate his work if his story were to be challenged. In his briefcase, he carried a portable fingerprinting device, and the FBI man was ready to match Boyle's print in the courtroom with the print on the document. Several of Sprague's associates urged him, the night before, to let Groenthal provide a dramatic finish to the trial, but the prosecutor declined. "Too much like Perry Mason," he said.

Charles Moses, well over six feet tall and with a head that seemed too small for his body, stood up in his freshly pressed gray suit, put his hands behind his back, and began to address the jury on behalf of his client, Tony Boyle.

"I feel that it is altogether fitting and proper," said Moses, "that this jury should be concerned about truth and justice in this particular week. The reason that I say that is that you all know that this is a week of suffering and pain, as you know. It is a Holy Week."

Moses's solemnity then degenerated into courtroom theatrics. He reached into a pocket, pulled out a stick of chalk, and began to rub it on his jacket.

"I don't know whether you can see that or not," Moses told the jurors. "But assume that you went to a local store to buy a new suit or a dress, and assume that the salesman brought out the dress or the suit and said to you, 'Here is a perfect fit, here is exactly what you should buy,' and on the suit lapel you see a big cigarette burn. The question is, would you buy that suit?"

The analogy to the prosecution case seemed far-fetched at best, and, considering the situation of Tony Boyle, embarrassing. For the rest of his closing speech to the jury, Moses was stuck with the chalk marks on his jacket, and as his voice lost strength in the stuffy late afternoon of the courtroom, some jurors' heads could be seen nodding. But Moses put up a strong battle.

He supported Boyle's testimony to the letter, and told the jurors they should be skeptical of the prosecution witnesses.

"That type of testimony," Moses said, "that Mr. Boyle said, 'Fine, go ahead and kill him,' does strike me as being a little

strange. Let me tell you a little bit about things that I think that
you ought to reasonably look for with respect to the testimony
in this case. If there was something of such a serious matter
discussed on the way downstairs, passing down the aisle or the
hallway, saying we ought to kill somebody, nobody will do it,
we will do it, okay, fine, and going on; if that is the way you
form a conspiracy to commit a murder, that is just a little
strange.

"And the reason that I say that is this. Let's assume that
somebody made a remark of that kind and that Mr. Turnblazer
and Mr. Pass were going back home. They would say to each
other, 'What in the hell was Tony Boyle talking about? Was he
serious? Did he want us to kill Yablonski? How are we going
to do it? What methods are we going to use? We are going to
have to talk to people.'

"Wouldn't there be some testimony, if someone came up to
you and said, 'Let's kill somebody,' and said it to two people,
that you might discuss it later, you might get together later and
say, 'What kind of a plan are we going to cook up? How are
we going to do that?'

"Wouldn't there even be some conversation sometime be-
tween Mr. Turnblazer and Mr. Pass about what in the hell was
Tony Boyle talking about? And there is none in this case.
None."

Moses also argued that if Prater's previous testimony was
to be believed, the conspiracy to murder Yablonski was formed
weeks before June 23, 1969.

The defense lawyer wound up by saying the evidence did
not support a guilty verdict.

"Since it is Holy Week," Moses added, "I have got two
quotations. 'Trust in a faithless man in time of trouble is like
a bad tooth or a foot that slips.' I didn't say it, I could never
come close to saying it in that fashion.

" 'When justice is done, it is a joy to the righteous and a
display to the evil doers.' . . . In this case I feel that a conviction
by this jury of Tony Boyle is one more step in conning the jury."

In the ten-minute recess that followed, Richard Sprague, entitled to the last word to the jury, marshaled his thoughts for what he regarded as the most important closing speech in his fifteen years of trial work.

The distance between the jury box and the defense table was about thirty feet. Moses had spoken to the jury from about twenty-five feet away, forcing him to elevate his none-too-powerful voice. Sprague could speak from anywhere in the courtroom and be heard, but he decided he would be most effective about five feet from the jury box. That, he reasoned, would insure rapport and intimacy between the prosecution and the panel. He would also be able to move about, back-pedaling when he wanted to point to the defendant, moving over to the prosecution table when he needed a piece of evidence. Sprague choreographed his speech so that no matter how long he spoke, the jury would rivet its attention on him.

"References to Holy Week, fine," Sprague told the jurors when they reassembled in their box. "What are they made to you for? In some way is that going to dissuade you as members of a jury from deciding this case and rendering justice? I trust not."

Sprague led the jury through definitions of legal terms—first-degree murder, second degree, manslaughter, malice—then began moving toward Boyle.

"I ask each of you to think in terms of motivation," he said. "Do you think a Silous Huddleston had the motivation? Look at this defendant, W.A. Tony Boyle."

A short pause while Sprague's right hand pointed at Boyle.

"He was the person that was heading that union. Who was Jock Yablonski attacking? Silous Huddleston? Prater? Albert Pass? Was Jock Yablonski trying to become the secretary-treasurer of District Nineteen? Was Jock Yablonski trying to become president of a little local? What position was Mr. Yablonski seeking? He was seeking the position that this defendant then occupied!"

Sprague showed contempt for the defense position that the main witnesses against Boyle were murderers and thieves.

"Well," he said, "who do you think this defendant is going to hire to assassinate? The Bishop of Boston? It is only ilk of this nature that you get to commit a crime like this."

Sprague said he had proved Boyle a liar in several instances, and exclaimed: "W.A. Tony Boyle—who has the gall to say to you, 'I never lie when I am under oath.' Lying isn't his big crime. Murder, assassination is his big crime.

"Now this defendant, the person who never lies under oath, this defendant Boyle says to you again so piously on the stand, I did not sit with Turnblazer on that plane, I sat with Carey, Ed Carey, I know it, I remember it, I always sat with him and I know I didn't sit with Turnblazer.

"Who is Carey? That was his lawyer in the United Mine Workers. Who else was with him on the plane? The lawyer that represented him before the grand jury, a fellow named Cacheris. You didn't see them produce Carey or Cacheris in here to support him that he was sitting on that plane with Carey. Not at all, because they knew it was a lie the moment it was uttered from the witness stand.

"But I guess they didn't think that we could get hold of anyone who was on that plane from last night until this morning. And who better to get hold of? Who better to get hold of than the woman who had been executive assistant for twenty years, who has no motivation to work with us? Who relates to you it was Turnblazer who sat with Boyle on that plane?"

For Boyle's offer of a $50,000 reward for the Yablonski murders, Sprague summoned his most scornful expression, which he turned toward Boyle as he said: "Members of the jury, as he said that to you he was dancing, he was laughing on the grave of his three victims."

For his peroration, Sprague commented that "defense counsel"—he never once mentioned Moses's name—had referred to the roads and trails of his native Montana.

"It has been a trail of assassination, a trail following murder," said Sprague quietly. And then, moving almost on top of Tony Boyle, the prosecutor concluded: "The trail, that long trail, leads to the originator of this crime. You know as every member here knows, the originator, the assassin himself is W.A. Tony Boyle, and your verdict should be guilty of murder in the first degree."

A hush came over the courtroom as Sprague sat down. Quietly the court stenographer finished tapping out Sprague's final words. Kenneth and Chip Yablonski sat in identical positions two rows behind the prosecution table; both were staring at the floor, hands clasped. At the defense table, Tony Boyle appeared at ease, and behind him, his wife and daughter could be seen whispering.

It was 4:32 P.M. In that hour-and-fifteen-minute address to the jury, Sprague seemed to have compressed more than four years of work.

It was too late in the day for Judge Catania to deliver his legal instructions, or charge, to the jury, so that was put off until the next morning. As the nine men and three women of the jury filed out to be locked up overnight for the last time, Sprague's steely eyes searched their faces for any possible indication of how his speech had gone over. Almost involuntarily, his right fist rapped three times on the wood of the prosecution table.

The jury received the case at 12:30 on the afternoon of Thursday, April 11. As Sprague had figured, the trial was going to be over before Good Friday. As always, he remained in the courthouse while the jurors deliberated. At four o'clock, there was a rush to the courtroom, but it turned out to be a false alarm, the jurors merely questioning a piece of evidence. Two hours later, Sprague sent out for his customary chocolate malted.

He never got to drink it. The jury came back at 6:15, and this time there was a verdict; but for ten minutes anticipation built up in the half-filled courtroom while the parties were located and notified to appear. Finally, from his perch on the bench, Judge Catania called for the clerk and stenographer.

Tony Boyle was brought in, looking pale but managing a wave to his family. His arm seemed weaker, as did he. Perhaps it was the lateness of the hour; perhaps he had missed his medication; or perhaps Tony Boyle was finally scared. He began sipping water from a paper cup and looked at the standing jurors.

"Will you take the verdict, please?" said the judge to the court clerk.

Clerk: Members of the jury, have you agreed upon a verdict?

Foreman: We have.

Clerk: In the issue joined between the Commonwealth of Pennsylvania and W.A. Tony Boyle, the defendant, do you find him guilty in the manner and form in which he stands indicted, or not guilty, as to Indictment Number One, March Sessions, 1974, Washington County, Number Six-fifty A 1973, charging him with the murder of Joseph Albert Yablonski?

Foreman: Guilty.

Clerk: And what is the degree?

Foreman: First.

The same ancient procedure was followed regarding the murders of Yablonski's wife and daughter, with the same out-come—guilty of murder in the first degree. All the jurors nodded their heads. Sitting beside Tony Boyle, attorney Charles Moses bowed his head, and supported it in his right hand for the balance of the proceedings.

When the jurors left, Moses asked for an extension of time to file a motion for a new trial. He wanted thirty days, but the rules of Pennsylvania courts allowed only a week. Sprague refused to agree to any extension. There were a few more minutes of legal arguments, over such issues as whether the exhibits would be physically available to the defense.

Judge Catania asked everyone to be seated while the defendant left. Boyle seemed to have found some reserve of strength that allowed him to leave the courtroom unassisted, after he took a final glance around the place where he had received his measure of justice. Moses hurried out with Boyle and disappeared down a back staircase.

The verdict produced no gloating from the prosecution side. Sprague said: "I fervently hope this verdict lets the public know that if they let their law-enforcement officials work and cooperate together without political interference, that cooperative law-enforcement agencies can take any event and trace it back—not just from the lower people at the bottom of the rung, but can trace it back to the people at the top, and successfully prosecute and convict them. It's about time that be done."

Afterword

FOR CHARLES "TIMER" MOSES the case of Tony Boyle was over, but the defense attorney faced one more proceeding in the big courtroom where Boyle had been convicted—a proceeding against himself. At 10:00 A.M. on Good Friday, the morning after Boyle's jury had returned its verdict, Moses confronted Richard Sprague and the president judge of the court, John V. Diggans. Moses stood accused of "indirect criminal contempt." Before Boyle's trial had begun, Moses had told a newspaper reporter that Boyle's private lie-detector test had proved "extremely favorable to the defendant." Incensed, Sprague had pressed the charge, arguing that Moses had violated an order covering material impounded by the court. Although Moses faced a maximum fine of one hundred dollars and fifteen days in jail, Sprague now told Judge Diggans, "I'd suggest to the court that there be no punishment." The prosecutor added, however, that Moses' conduct should not be condoned.

Judge Diggans frowned. Indirect criminal contempt (meaning that the offense occurred outside of the courtroom) is a rare charge. In the nearly empty courtroom, the judge rambled on about not being the sort of jurist who admonishes or lectures attorneys. Finally, conceding that no purpose would be served by a harsh decision, Diggans sentenced Moses to pay a nominal fine of one dollar. Moses, red-faced, said not a word to the court or to his attorney. He rushed down a back staircase and was off to his native Montana, never again to represent his old friend Tony Boyle.

Jock Yablonski's two sons invited twenty-five persons to a restored eighteenth-century inn several hours after Tony Boyle's conviction. In a private dining room, the candlelit tables were arranged in a *U*. At the head were Richard Sprague and Ken and Chip Yablonski, surrounded by FBI agents, Pennsylvania state policemen, and several of Sprague's detectives. Now that it was over, there was little joy, but neither was it all grim. There were toasts to Sprague and the other law-enforcement people; there were off-the-record speeches; there was some banter, and several times Jock Yablonski's name was recalled with reverence; but none of the speakers mentioned Tony Boyle. The dinner and talk went on until midnight. Sprague, somewhat embarrassed by all the attention, said later, "I feel a little bit like the guest at the Last Supper." When I asked Sprague if the Yablonski case would be his swan song in the Philadelphia district attorney's office (where a new D.A. had been elected a few months earlier), Sprague said, "No, no swan song. I'll still be swinging in that office."

But he was wrong. A lifelong Democrat whose political hero was Franklin D. Roosevelt, Sprague had worked for a Republican district attorney for eight years, had been appointed special prosecutor in the Yablonski case by a Republican administration in Pennsylvania, and had cooperated throughout with President Nixon's Department of Justice. Somehow, Sprague had managed to keep politics out of the case. But now a fellow-Democrat and local politics gave Sprague his first comeuppance in public life.

From the start of F. Emmett Fitzpatrick's administration as district attorney of Philadelphia, it was clear that he and Sprague were not going to work well together. Fitzpatrick, a big, bluff man who had been a successful criminal lawyer, wanted total control of the office; Sprague, serious about his duties and a veteran of the office, had been accustomed to the role of day-to-day chief executive officer. Moreover, Sprague was identified with the political forces of Philadelphia Mayor Frank Rizzo, who had opposed Fitzpatrick for D.A. Fitz-

patrick, controversial and outspoken, was a longtime friend of
Sprague's, but he was not awed by the special prosecutor's
national fame in the Yablonski case.

When Fitzpatrick got into hot water over political contributions to his election campaign, Sprague started talking about the
integrity of the D.A.'s office. At first covertly and then publicly,
Sprague questioned his boss's conduct on other matters. Finally,
things came to a head when Sprague charged publicly that
Fitzpatrick had recommended a lenient sentence for a convicted
blackmailer whom Fitzpatrick had represented in private practice. Sprague accused Fitzpatrick of lying about the case. Fitzpatrick demanded Sprague's resignation. Sprague refused to
quit. In December 1974, with only a few hours' notice, Fitzpatrick fired his first assistant. Richard Sprague's public career,
spanning seventeen years in the Philadelphia district attorney's
office, was over. Soon after, at the age of fifty, Sprague set up
his shingle in the unaccustomed but more lucrative world of
private law practice in Philadelphia.

While all this was going on, Sprague remained as special
prosecutor in the Yablonski murder case. Several months after
Tony Boyle's conviction, Sprague asked a federal court to go
easy on William Turnblazer, the former UMW District 19 president whose testimony had been instrumental in convicting
Boyle. Pennsylvania murder charges against Turnblazer were
dropped, and he was given a five-to-fifteen-year term in a federal
prison. Sprague revealed that Turnblazer had never asked for
immunity from prosecution but that he would have been
granted it had he so requested. Turnblazer wound up in a federal
facility in Maryland where some of the Watergate defendants
were housed. He could be paroled as early as 1978.

Annette Gilly and her father Silous Huddleston got the
strangest deal of all. In the summer of 1974, Washington County
Judge Charles Sweet gave them credit for the four years' confinement they had already served—most of that time in motels
and on farms. Then he freed them under federal auspices.

The two confessed conspirators were released in circumstances normally reserved for underworld figures who turn evidence against mobsters. They were given new identities and spirited to a place known only to a handful of law-enforcement officers. Their only legal obligation was ten years' probation. Justifying the leniency, Sprague told Judge Sweet: "If they had not talked, Boyle and other higher-ups still would be enjoying the comforts of a free existence, and justice would not have been done." He also said that the secret identities were necessary to protect Annette and her father from reprisal.

Left behind in various Pennsylvania prisons were Mrs. Gilly's husband Paul, Claude Vealey, Aubran Martin, Albert Pass, and William Prater. Only Prater, serving a federal sentence of life for his cooperation, could look forward to the chance of eventual freedom.

On September 11, 1975, the Court of Common Pleas of Delaware County, Criminal Division, completed its action in *Commonwealth of Pennsylvania* vs. *W. A. Boyle* by sentencing the seventy-three-year-old defendant to three life terms for the murders of Joseph, Margaret, and Charlotte Yablonski.

Boyle's only words to the court were: "All I can say is I'm innocent."

Index